Multiple Penetrating Attacks for Winning Basketball

Multiple Penetrating Attacks for Winning Basketball

by Frank Zampardi

Parker Publishing Company, Inc.

West Nyack, New York

Library of Congress Cataloging in Publication Data

Zampardi, Frank
   Multiple penetrating attacks for winning basketball.

   Includes index.
   1. Basketball--Offense. 2. Basketball coaching.
I. Title.
GV889.Z35   796.32'32   79-16143
ISBN 0-13-604934-6

Dedication

I dedicate this book to my beautiful daughters, Heather and Danielle, and to my wife Janice, who gave me the inspiration to produce this work.

Acknowledgments

I would like to acknowledge the following people who aided or shared their knowledge with me:

Bob Barrett, Athletic Director at Chadwicks High School, for his cooperation and guidance.

Jean Prime and Rosemary Facchini, for their assistance in preparing this manuscript.

Bob Devins, Head Basketball Coach at Notre Dame High School, for sharing his tremendous knowledge of basketball and for making me an integral part of the Notre Dame basketball program.

All the athletes I have worked with. Their desire and dedication have made coaching an exciting and rewarding experience.

The late Joseph E. Jursak, former principal at Chadwicks, who gave me my first coaching appointment.

What This Book Will Do for You

If you want to develop offensive proficiency, you'll find this book invaluable. It contains fresh material with a unique approach to offensive basketball. If the conventional patterns are not suitable to your personnel from year to year, this multiple offensive system will help.

At the high school level, so much time is spent on coaching skills and fundamentals that there is often little time left to coach special situations and develop an offense that can be used to combat the man-to-man, different zones and combination zone defenses. As sophisticated as basketball is today, most high school coaches, even with "blue-chip" players, never seem to have enough preparation time before their season openers.

After having tried some of the proven offenses with varying degrees of success, we decided we really needed a system of penetrating attacks that would:

(1)   be workable against any defense.
(2)   provide more than one option for the best shooters.
(3)   provide the weaker shooters high-percentage shots.
(4)   provide excellent offensive rebounding position.
(5)   allow all five players a chance to score.
(6)   create mismatches.
(7)   have floor balance.
(8)   allow adequate transition from offense to defense.
(9)   allow more time for coaching defense and special situations.
(10) be easy to teach.
(11) be simple enough to be learned quickly and executed easily by the younger players.
(12) eliminate confusion and ensure sound execution.
(13) make substitution easy because all five players have developed a workable knowledge of all formations.

The multiple penetrating attack offense is executed from any of four alignments: The Basic Inside-Out, High 1-4, Double Low Stack, and a Spread 1-2-2. From any of these formations (depending on defensive tactics), the selected alignment can attack the defense with identical options and simultaneously present the defense with a different look. Positioning of the alignment and offensive player movement are keys in keeping the defense off-balance.

There are 24 scoring options in each of the four formations used, thus presenting the defense with what could be 96 explosive scoring threats. These multiple formations are possible and not confusing to the offensive players because the options are the same regardless of the formation that is attacking the defense.

This book shows you how to make offensive pressure just as potent a weapon as defensive pressure. Each entry pass is received in a high-percentage scoring area, providing you with close-in power shots, the fifteen-foot jumper and fantastic offensive rebounding position needed for the all-important second shot. Solid offensive rebounding is vital to the success of any offense.

The Multiple Penetrating System is so versatile that it can be used against the man-to-man, zones or combination defenses, without complicated adjustments. It is adaptable to any level of competition, it can be added to your present offensive system or it can be used as your basic offense. Its flexibility provides for free-lance possibilities, thus eliminating any stereotyping of the patterned offenses.

The Basic Inside-Out Attack in Chapter 1 is the heart of the material. It may be used against any of basketball's defenses. This attack allows you to take a blend of average and below average players, utilize their strengths and mold them into a strong unit that will enable you to overcome opponents who have superior height and talent.

The Clear-Out Series in Chapter 2 enables you to take advantage of a talented offensive player. This unusual alignment creates many one-on-one opportunities and a powerful inside game, because it completely distorts the defense and its coverage.

Special attention is given to attacking zones and combination defenses in Chapter 5. Emphasis is placed on understanding zone defenses. For example, the movements of the Standard Sliding Zones and the Stunting Zones are discussed, and methods of countering them are given. Offensive principles such as spreading the zone, getting behind the zone and tactics used to keep an active post are explained. Fundamental concepts for dealing with the zone such as developing passing angles, ball reversal maneuvers, types of cuts and methods for penetration are covered. Techniques for establishing an inside game versus the zone are also discussed in detail. Another feature of this chapter is a section on solving the matchup defenses with a 1-3-1 Passing Game. Drills, advantages, rules for passing and dribbling and post- and perimeter-player rules necessary for the development of this free-lance offense are included. Methods for attacking the Box-and-one, Diamond-and-one, and the Triangle-and-two are also described.

Teams that use the 1-3-1 zone defense have created many problems for conventional offenses. Chapter 6 deals exclusively with a 1-4 penetrating attack against the 1-3-1. This chapter describes methods for creating 2-on-1 situations against the 1-3-1, techniques that force the baseline defender out and strategies for penetrating the low-post area.

Chapter 7 on coaching the controlled fast break with penetration offers a well-conceived and coordinated transitional fast-break offensive attack that provides scoring opportunities for each player. The controlled fast break places the ball in the hands of your best ballhandler who controls the break. This chapter includes ten advantages of the controlled fast break, organization, personnel requirements and the explosive scoring swing-pass series.

The book includes over 50 drills for the development of offensive proficiency and the multiple penetrating attack offense. Multiple scoring plays from special situations and last-second offenses aid in making this an explosive offensive scoring machine.

Frank Zampardi

Contents

What This Book Will Do for You 7

1. Installing the Basic Inside-Out Penetrating Attack 21

   The Inside-Out Versus Any Defense

   Personnel Placement and Description

   Multiple Formation Potential
      The Strongside
      Versatility of the Offense

   Initiating the Basic Inside-Out Attack with Guard Entries
      Hitting the Wing
      Hitting the Side Post
      Hitting the Stack
         Proper Footwork in Screening

   Basic Continuity and Offensive Moves
      Penetrating the Low Post
      Executing the Pick-and-Roll
      Undercutting with the Wing Guard
      Getting into the Baseline Series
         "Jam-It" to the Big Man
         Post Roll-and-Exchange
         Guard Through
         Double Low-Stack Alignment

   Attacking the Weakside with Penetration
      Hitting the Stack
      Reversing to the Wing

Relieving Guard Pressure
    Wing-Guard Screen
    Post Screen-and-Roll
    Backdoor Series

End-of-Period Offense
    Rotating into the Stack
    The "Quick Popper"

Rebound Responsibility

Drills for the Basic Inside-Out Attack
    Pick-and-Roll
    Hitting the Stack
    Baseline Series

2. A Clear-Out Series for Your Best Shooter 45

An Auxiliary Man-for-Man Attack

Take Advantage of a Weak Defense

Relieve Guard Pressure
    Two-Man Pick-and-Roll
    Posting Low
    Backdoor

Continuity Pattern
    Clear-Out
    Scissor

Reverse Action

3. Penetrating the Man-for-Man Defense with a 1-4 Attack.. 57

Alignment

Establishing a Strongside

Executing the Pick-and-Roll (Coming-Over-the-Top)

Getting into the Baseline Series with the 1-4
    Reversing to the Weakside
    Strongside Post Roll-and-Exchange

Getting into the Baseline Series from the High Post
Guard Clear (Rub Off the Post)
Backdoor Series (Hitting the High Post)
Rebound Responsibilities
Fundamental Factors for Offensive Rebounding

4. The Double Low-Stack and the Spread 1-2-2 69

Getting into the Stack
Advantages of the Stack
Disadvantages of the Stack
Offensive Keys
Establishing a Strongside
Screening by the Post Man
"Jamming-It" to the Low Post
Pick-and-Roll
Weakside Cut Over-the-Top
Getting into the Baseline Series
Post Roll-and-Exchange
Reversing to the Wing
Relieving Guard Pressure
Rebound Responsibilities
The Spread 1-2-2—Basic Formation
Open Key Advantages
Strongside Entries
Guard to Wing Guard
Guard to Post
Weakside Entries
Identical Keys
Backdoor
Relieving Pressure
Rebound Responsibilities

The Spread 1-2-2 Delay-Game Offense
Advantages of the Spread Pattern
When to Use the Delay-Game Offense
Rules for the Delay-Game Offense
Alignment and Continuity

5   Attacking Zone Defenses with Multiple Penetrating Attacks   89

Zone Offense
Suggested Factors for Team Play Versus Zone Defenses

Types of Zone Defenses
The Standard Sliding Zones
The Laning or Stunting Zones
Combination Zones
Zone Presses

Offensive Principles Versus Zone Defenses

Fundamanetal Concepts Versus Zone Defenses
Passing
Overloading and Triangular Passing
Developing Passing Lanes
Ball-Reversal Maneuver (Screening Baseline)
Pressure the High and Low Posts
Penetration Against the Zones
Types of Cuts

Formations Against the Various Zones
The Basic Inside-Out Offense Versus Even-Front Zones
Point to Wing Guard
Getting into the Baseline Series
Post Roll-and-Exchange
Reversing to the Wing
Weakside Step-In
Weakside Series
"Jam-It" to the Big Man
Guard Cut

Spotting Up

Meeting the Combination Zones

The Matchup Zones

1-3-1 Passing-Game Offense Versus Matchup Defense

Passing Rules

Dribble Rules

General Rules

Post-Player Rules

Perimeter Player Rules

Teaching the Passing Game with Drills

Pass-Screen Opposite Drill

Step-In or Replace Drill

Post-Screen Post Drill

Rear-Screen Continuity Drill

Scrimmage Games

The Box-and-One, Diamond-and-One and the Triangle-and-Two

Attacking the Combinations

The Stack Versus the Box-and-One

6.   A Penetrating 1-4 Versus the 1-3-1 Zone Defense 117

Popularity of the 1-3-1 Zone Defense

Meeting and Countering the 1-3-1 Zone Defense

Advantages of the 1-4 Against the 1-3-1

Guard Entries

Pass to the Strongside Wing

Pass to the Weakside Wing

Pass to the Strongside Post

Pass to the Weakside Post

Guard Cut

100 Series

Pass to the Wing Guard

Pass to the Pivot

Rebound Responsibilities

7. Coaching the Controlled Fast Break with Penetration 127

Psychological Effect on the Opposition

Advantages of the Controlled Fast Break

Organizing the Controlled Fast Break
Starting the Controlled Fast Break
Fast-Break Factors
Personnel Requirements
Advantage Situation
Non-Advantage Situation
Alley
Swing-Pass Series

Drills for Developing the Controlled Fast Break
Fast-Break Progression Drill
Three-Man Progression Drill
Four-Man Series
Five-Man Fast Break

Fundamental Drills for the Controlled Fast Break
Drill for Player 1
Three-on-Two, Two-on-One Drill
Round-Robin Drill
Head-Pass Drill
Change-of-Direction Drill
11-Man Continuity Drill

8. Attacking Pressure Defenses with Multiple Penetrating
Attacks 151

The Use of Pressure Defenses

Psychological Outlook Against the Press

Principles for Ball Advancement Versus Pressing Defenses
Ball Advancement Principles
Zone-Press Offensive Tempo
Keys for Defeating Zone Presses

Zone-Press Offense

    Basic Alignments

    Guard Cut

    Weakside Flash

    Pass to the Safety

    Swing Series

    Guard Cut from the Stack Alignment

Attacking Full-Court Man-for-Man Pressure

    1-4 Attack Versus Man-for-Man Full-Court Pressure

    Swing Series

    Double-Option Bomb

Attacking Half-Court Pressure

    The 1-4 Versus Half-Court Man-for-Man Pressure

    The 1-4 Versus Half-Court Zone Pressure

9.   Special Situation Plays with Multiple Penetrating Attacks   177

Scoring Plays from Out-of-Bounds

    Player Positions

    Horizontal

    Stack

    Vertical

    Box

    A Successful Side-Out Series

        Four-Option Continuity Play

        Half-Court Last-Second Shot

Full-Court Last-Second Shot Versus Man-for-Man Pressure

    The Home Run

Practice Organization

    The Special

Multiple-Scoring Plays from the Jump-Ball

    Basic Rules on Jump-Balls

    The Box Screen-Opposite Tap

The Diamond Double-Screen

The Y-Formation and Fast Break

The Squeeze

10.   Drills for Developing Offensive Proficiency 193

The Importance of Fundamentals

Non-Dribble Series

Fingertip Passing

Circle the Body

Circling Each Leg Separately

Figure Eight

Switch

Front-to-Back Bounce-Catch

Ball in Front

Ball Between Legs

Slap the Thighs

Dribble Series

Whirl-Around

Double-Dribble

Dribble-Reverse and Pivot

Four-Corner Dribble, Pivot and Pass

Dribble, Jump-Stop, Pivot and Pass

Full-Court Reverse-Dribble

Cross-Over Dribble and Shoot

Full-Speed Spin, Dribble and Shoot

Rocker-Step and Drive

Jab-Step and Drive

Passing

Two-Line Passing

Rapid-Fire Passing

Wall-Pass Catching

Four-Corner Dribble, Pivot and Pass

Four-Corner Passing

Four-Corner Pass and Shoot

Four-Man Passing

Full-Court Head Passing

Full-Court Press-Breaker Pass-and-Cut

Pass-and-Shoot

Four-Corner Pass-and-Shoot

Change-of-Direction Move, Pass-and-Shoot

Big Man

Layups

Speed-Dribble with Power Layups

Reverse Layup

Reverse-Dribble and Layup

Full-Court Layups

Shooting

Three-Line Dribble, Pass and Shoot

Follow Your Shot

Competitive Shooting

Drive and Jump-Shot

Nine-Minute Shooting

Index. 221

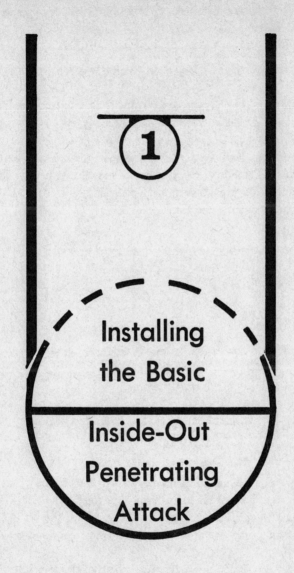

1

Installing the Basic Inside-Out Penetrating Attack

The Inside-Out Offense Versus Any Defense

The Inside-Out is an offense that is effective against any defense without making complicated adjustments. "Stunting" defenses with varying amounts of pressure from the man-for-man, zones, combination zones and full-court presses have been successful against many offenses. Realizing that you can be confronted with these tactics, you need to develop an effective attack that makes use of the talents and skills of *your* personnel in order to establish parity with stronger opponents.

Personnel Placement and Description

Diagram 1-1 illustrates the Basic Inside-Out Attack formation. Player 1 is the point man and is responsible for initiating either the strongside or weakside attack. He should be a good one-on-one player, be able to penetrate to the basket and shoot the power layup and possess excellent passing and ball handling skills. He should also possess good court savvy, being able to "read" the defense and make the correct entry pass. In addition, he should be an excellent defender against the fast break.

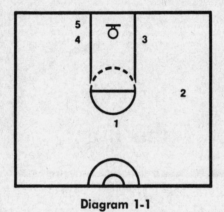

Diagram 1-1

In order to help your point men bring the ball up-court as quickly as possible, before the defense can react, emphasize the following dribble maneuvers: the reverse or spin, the stutter, the stop-and-go, the behind-the-back, the change-of-direction, the outside push, the cross-over and the change-of-pace.

Player 2 is the most important player in all of the multiple attacks. He should be your best all-around player, have the ability to make the 15-to-18-foot jump-shot and the ability to move without the ball. He should be a good ball handler and passer in working the two- and three-man game, an excellent penetrator with good power moves in close and an aggressive offensive and defensive rebounder. In addition, when using the footwork and cutting techniques of the motion offense, player 2 should be able to read defensive mistakes in order to free himself and should be schooled in the proper use of screens. He should also assist in relieving pressure on the point guard.

Player 2 should be your second biggest guard or smaller quick forward. For the most part, he leads the outside game against zone defenses. You should also expect player 2 to be an aggressive defensive rebounder and to help fill the lanes when you have the opportunity to fast break.

Player 3 is your best big man, rebounder and inside scorer. He must be an adequate shooter from 10 to 15 feet and a strong performer in close. He should be an aggressive offensive and defensive rebounder with good hands and passing ability. For the most part, he leads the inside game and must work well with players 1 and 2.

Note that player 3 is positioned midway between the baseline and the free-throw line. We refer to him as a side post and have found that it is difficult for opponents to defend him from this position. From this spot he has room to maneuver to his right or left without being too concerned about getting off-the-ball help from other defenders.

Player 4 has a less spectacular responsibility in the multiple attacks, although it is possibly one of the most important. He must be drilled in setting solid screens for the better shooters. It is an absolute must that he be an aggressive *offensive* rebounder and that he possess a respectable inside game for the success of your attacks. Most of the shots in your attacks occur opposite player 4 and fall to his side. We refer to him as the "garbage man" because 75 percent of his scoring results from the all-important second shot. The only real criterion for this position is that the player has the desire to rebound.

Player 5 is stacked with player 4 and should be your second-best medium-range shooter. He need not be a big player and could possibly be a guard or small forward who is a reasonably good shooter from 10 feet. He should be a good one-on-one player, a good passer and have good court savvy in order to establish a two-man game with player 4. In addition, he should be able to move well without the ball, since he duplicates some of the responsibilities of player 2.

Multiple Formation Potential

The Strongside

We refer to the strongside in the Basic Inside-Out Attack as the side where players 2 and 3 are positioned. Diagram 1-2 shows that player 3 is on the side post and player 2 is on the right wing. This establishes the strongside. As soon as the point guard carries the ball to the strongside, a natural triangle is formed with players 1, 2 and 3. (Diagram 1-3)

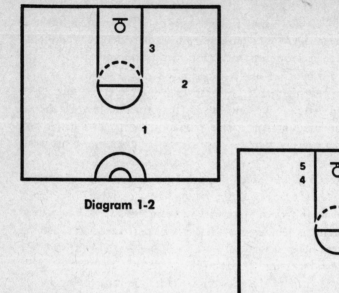

Diagram 1-2

Diagram 1-3

Versatility of the Offense

The Basic Inside-Out Attack has proven its versatility by adapting to any defense faced. Its multiple look has posed many problems for opponents because it constantly forces the defense to operate in unfamiliar areas. The constant application of offensive pressure has consistently kept the defense off balance.

It should be noted that in describing the execution of the Basic Inside-Out Attack, the only physical adjustment in the offense is the execution of a pick-and-roll maneuver between players 2 and 3.

When facing a zone with a two guard front, you should eliminate the pick-and-roll option, and try to hit player 2 in the open-wing area instead. He can shoot or look for player 3 in the side-post area before cutting under the zone. Attacking zone defenses with the Inside-Out is explained in Chapter 5.

Note how the Basic Inside-Out Attack distorts a 2-3 zone in Diagram 1-4. Defensive players X3 and X5 must each defend against two offensive players. Player X4 and either X1 or X2 are wasted by not having an offensive player to contend with. You will be able to slip through the gaps in zone defenses for many offensive rebounds. This constant 2-on-1 pressure versus the zone makes this an explosive attack!

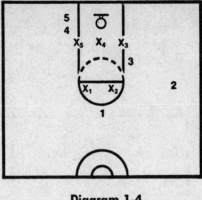

Diagram 1-4

Diagrams 1-5 and 1-6 illustrate how versatile the Basic Inside-Out Attack is in creating a multiple-formation look.

By placing player 2 behind player 3, as in Diagram 1-5, you change to the popular double low-stack offense which can establish a very explosive inside game with players 3 and 4 close to the basket.

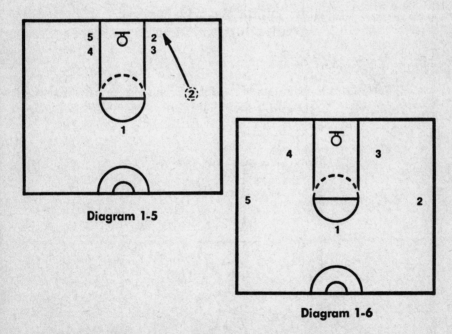

Diagram 1-5

Diagram 1-6

By pulling player 5 out and opposite player 2, as in Diagram 1-6, you develop the Spread 1-2-2 or Passing-Game Attack.

Diagram 1-7 illustrates how easy it is to get into a 1-4 offense. The simple adjustment of players 3 and 4 to a high position accomplishes the conversion nicely.

Dropping player 4 down low, as in Diagram 1-8, gives you a 1-3-1 Offensive Attack.

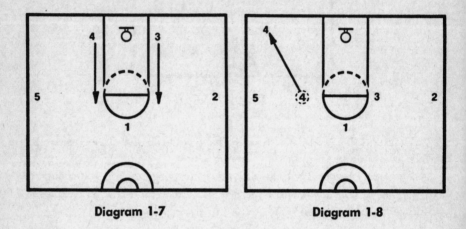

Diagram 1-7   Diagram 1-8

Initiating the Basic Inside-Out Attack with Guard Entries

Hitting the Wing

In Diagram 1-9, point guard 1 dribbles to his left, reverses his dribble and crosses over or uses any maneuver he can use to beat his man. Then player 1 hits player 2, who makes a change-of-direction move to receive the pass.

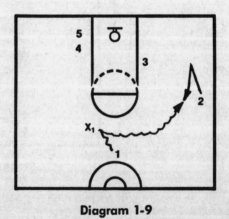

Diagram 1-9

Player 2 receives this pass with a hard jump-stop. You should teach your players to catch passes with a jump-stop, then "shape up" into a low triple-threat position (able to pass, to drive or to shoot). Coming to a jump-stop allows your players to establish *two* pivot feet and then pivot *into* the defensive man and not away from the basket. By executing a front-pivot, you are attacking the defense within scoring range. The reverse-pivot can place an offensive player four feet or more further out and, in all probability, out of scoring range. Diagram 1-10 illustrates the incorrect way and Diagram 1-11 illustrates the correct way of "shaping up." In Diagram 1-11, the pivot is executed on the player's *inside* foot, and the outside foot is swung completely around so that the player is facing the basket.

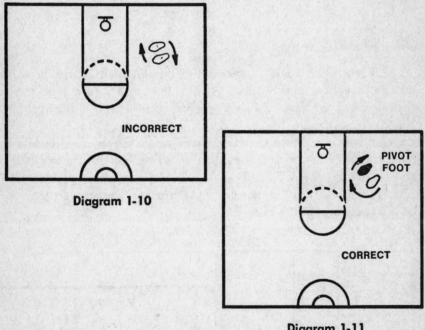

Diagram 1-10

Diagram 1-11

After "shaping up" into the triple-threat position, Player 2 can hit player 3 in the low-post position by passing *away* from the defensive man as seen in Diagram 1-12. He can also shoot or work his man one-on-one as close to the basket as possible in order to get off a high-percentage shot. If player 2 elects to penetrate, player 3 vacates and fills an open area, which eliminates any defensive help on player 2. (Diagram 1-13) As illustrated in Diagram 1-12, player 1, after passing to player 2, moves toward him as a safety by using a change-of-direction move on his defender.

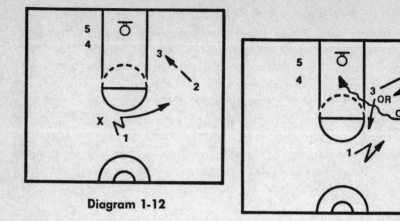

Diagram 1-12

Diagram 1-13

Hitting the Side Post

Placing player 3 midway between the baseline and the free-throw line adds more pressure on the defense. As you can see in Diagram 1-14, there is little defensive help available on player 3 from either side of the free-throw lane. If the point guard has any difficulty in getting the ball to player 2 when the strongside is established, player 3 can flash high and provide another entry for the point guard. It should be apparent that the backdoor, with players 2 and 3, would now be available. (Diagram 1-15) Player 3 comes up high and 2, using a change-of-direction move, cuts to the basket. The backdoor series will be discussed later in this chapter.

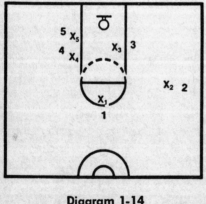

Diagram 1-14

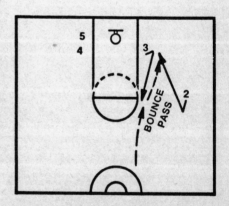

Diagram 1-15

Hitting the Stack

The last point of entry for the point guard is to hit the stack on the weakside. In this sequence, footwork by the screener, player 4, is extremely important; so important that you should review it nearly every day throughout the season. Constant emphasis on correct screening techniques will allow your best shooters to get open and take advantage of high-percentage shots.

Proper Footwork in Screening. The stack is aligned so that the players in tandem are facing the ball. As soon as the point guard decides to attack the weakside, player 5 taps player 4, signaling him to screen player 5's defensive man. This screening maneuver is executed in a 135-degree turn by player 4 as he pivots on his *outside* foot (right), swings his other foot around as if stepping backward and faces player 5's defensive man. Player 5 rubs shoulders with player 4 and loses his man long enough to receive the pass from the point guard. As soon as player 5 rubs shoulders, player 4 completes a 360-degree turn on his right foot by swinging his left leg around and, while facing the ball again, looks for a pass from the point guard. This maneuver is very successful, especially when the defense switches. This is also an excellent maneuver against zone defenses when the bottom outside defender breaks the screen set by player 4, leaving player 4 open for a pass and power-move to the inside.

Diagrams 1-16 to 1-20 illustrate this screening technique and subsequent "explosion" to the ball by player 4.

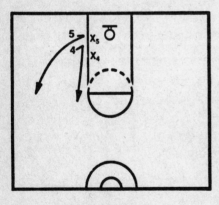

Diagram 1-16
Screen set by 4

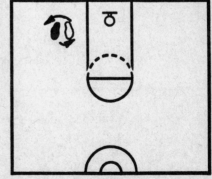

Diagram 1-17
Start of pivot

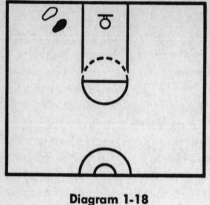

Diagram 1-18
135-degree turn

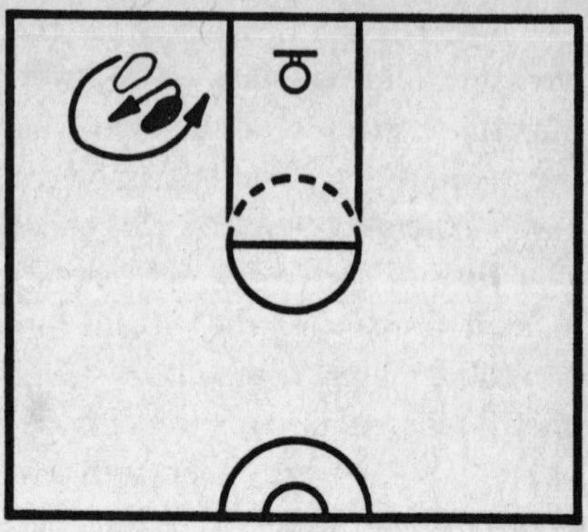

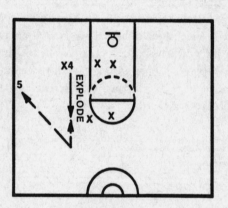

Diagram 1-19
360-degree turn

Diagram 1-20
Player 4 "explodes" to the ball

Basic Continuity and Offensive Moves

Penetrating the Low Post

The basic entries and offensive moves have been described. Let's see how the continuity develops from the Basic Inside-Out Attack with penetration in the low-post areas.

The first offensive sequence begins with the entry pass from point guard 1 to the wing 2. Player 2 can shoot, hit the post man, player 3, or penetrate one-on-one to the basket.

Executing the Pick-and-Roll

If the wing guard, player 2, is having difficulty scoring from his basic position, the attack is varied with the execution of a pick-and-roll between players 2 and 3. Upon sensing the pass from the point guard, player 2 signals player 3 to set a pick for him. If the defense switches (and you want them to) a mismatch is created so that a smaller defensive player has the responsibility of handling your post man. (Diagram 1-21)

If 2 elects to penetrate or shoot over the screen set by 3, player 3 follows for the all-important rebound. If 2 does not have this high-percentage shot on the drive or the jump-shot, and if he cannot hit 3 on the roll, player 2 passes back to 1 who has filled in as the safety and continues across the baseline. (Diagram 1-22)

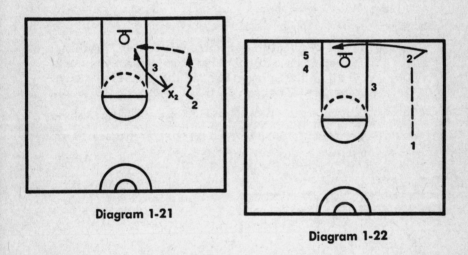

Diagram 1-21

Diagram 1-22

Undercutting with the Wing Guard

Diagram 1-23 illustrates how the continuity is maintained. As soon as player 5 sees 2 return the ball to 1, he taps the weakside post man, player 4, signaling him to screen 5's defensive man. The point guard, 1, then dribbles the ball left, looking for 5 who is coming toward the ball looking for the pass and short jumper.

> **NOTE:** Player 5 should receive this pass just as he enters the free-throw lane so that he can turn and shoot directly in front of the basket or hit 4, who has by now "exploded" to the ball with his defender on his back. If he doesn't receive the ball, he clears through.

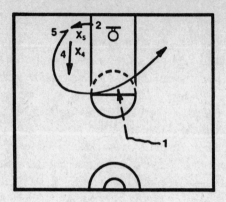

Diagram 1-23

If player 5 hits 4 low, player 4 must make a quick, strong power-move because he may be caught for a three-second violation.

NOTE: Player 1 should <u>never</u> force this pass to 5 against a zone defense. He should look immediately to 4 or 2. Both of these players are "splitting" the low defensive man. (Diagram 1-24)

Wing guard 2 has been cutting under the defense, and if neither 5 nor 4 is open in this sequence, player 1 can look for 2, who will rub shoulders with 4 as he pops out to receive this pass. (Diagram 1-25)

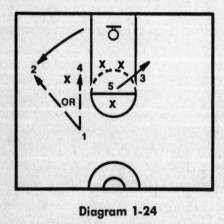

Diagram 1-24

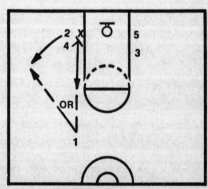

Diagram 1-25

In the meantime, 5 has cut through or under the defense and has stacked with 3 on the opposite side of the lane.

NOTE: You should always have a big man low in anticipation of the offensive rebound.

A potential backdoor situation exists with players 2 and 4. Player 4, who has come high, can pivot upon receipt of the ball from 1 and can hit 2 cutting to the basket. (Diagram 1-26)

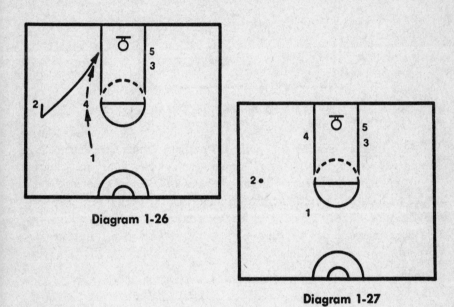

Diagram 1-26

Diagram 1-27

Getting into the Baseline Series

With 2 having come across the key and with possession of the ball, begin the Baseline Series with your best shooter handling the ball and a big man, player 4, in low near the basket. (Diagram 1-27)

"Jam-it" to the Big Man. Wing guard 2 has the identical options on this side of the key with player 4 as he had earlier with player 3. However, you really want 2 to "jam-it" deep to player 4, for the close-in power shot.

Post Man Roll-and-Exchange. If 2 cannot shoot or hit 4 low, player 4 clears out across the lane, allowing 3, your best big man, to move high and then roll low along the free-throw lane. Player 3 receives the pass from 2 for a short jumper or the drive for the close-in power shot. This option is especially effective against man-for-man and zone defenses. The success of this option is based on the fact that 3 can move between the front-line and back-line defenders of a zone, and he can move against a man-for-man defense because he is heading toward the ball with his defender on his back. (Diagram 1-28)

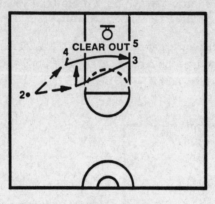

Diagram 1-28

Guard Through. At this point in the Basic Inside-Out Penetrating Attack, the point guard, player 1, has not been involved in any real scoring opportunities. This becomes a blessing because 1's defender becomes preoccupied with watching the action away from him. If the wing guard, player 2, has possession of the ball and is unable to hit 3 on his roll, player 1, reading his defender's mistake, can cut through for any easy layup as illustrated in Diagram 1-29.

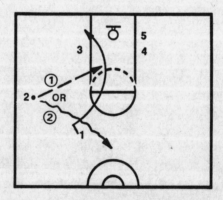

Diagram 1-29

If 1 cannot receive this pass from 2, he cuts left and stacks with 3. Player 2, meanwhile, brings the ball out to the top of the key. (Diagram 1-29)

Double Low-Stack Alignment. Diagram 1-30 shows the Basic Inside-Out Attack in a double low-stack alignment. Player 2, now working the opposite side of the court, hits 5 as he pops out from behind 4. Player 5 can shoot, hit 4 low, execute a pick-and-roll with 4 or pass back to 2. If 5 elects to pass back to 2, player 2 can work his man one-on-one or dribble left and hit 1 coming off a screen set by player 3. Player 1 has the identical options as 4 and 5 had on the opposite side. After passing to 1, players 2 and 5 exchange positions. (Diagram 1-31)

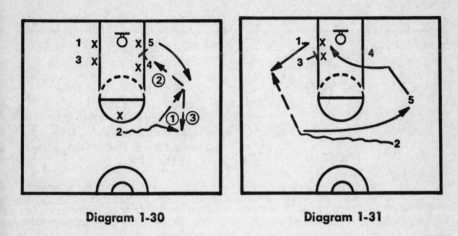

Diagram 1-30   **Diagram 1-31**

If player 1 elects to dribble back to the point, players 5, 3, 4 and 2 return to their original positions.

All of the previous action occurred when 1 initiated the attack to player 2. Let's see what happens if the point guard starts the offense on the weakside.

Attacking the Weakside with Penetration

Hitting the Stack

In the following illustrations you will see that the Basic Inside-Out Attack, when initiated from the weakside, will revert to the baseline series options or the post man roll-and-exchange option.

In Diagram 1-32, player 1 starts the attack by hitting 5 who taps 4 and rubs shoulders with him to receive the pass. Player 5 can shoot, "jam-it" low to 4 or execute a pick-and-roll with 4. (Diagram 1-33) If none of these options are available, player 4 clears out and 3 moves high and then rolls low, looking for a pass from 5. (Diagram 1-33)

Diagram 1-32

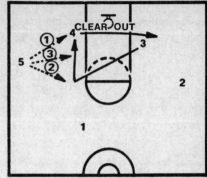

Diagram 1-33

COACHING POINT: Instruct your players that anytime they handle the ball in the point position, they <u>must</u> dribble the ball to the side they select for an entry pass. It is too risky to pass the ball to the wings from the top of the key.

Another variation with this sequence is that 1 can head-hunt 2's man, allowing 2 to come over the top for a 15-footer from the foul line. After screening for 2, 1 replaces himself at the point in case 5 could not execute any of his options. (Diagram 1-34) If 5 returns the ball to the point man, he and 2 stack with the two big men opposite them. (Diagram 1-35)

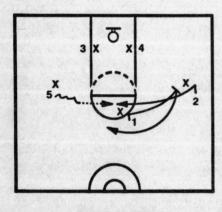

Diagram 1-34

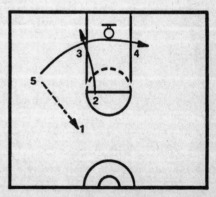

Diagram 1-35

Reversing to the Wing

At this point, player 1 can now reverse the ball to his right and hit 5 coming off a screen from 4. (Diagram 1-36) Player 4 can "explode" to the ball as he and 5 "split" the defense. The pick-and-roll is available; player 5 can "jam-it" low, and player 2 can come over the top as the continuity is maintained.

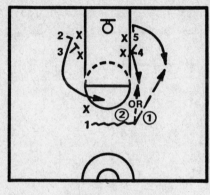

Diagram 1-36

Relieving Guard Pressure

Wing Guard Screen

If the point guard is having difficulty with pressure from his defender, you can relieve this pressure by having the wing guard, player 2, set a screen on 1's man. As 1 and 2 exchange, the offense can be executed with 1 now working with 3. (Diagram 1-37)

Diagram 1-37

Post Screen-and-Roll

Another variation to relieve guard pressure is to create a mismatch with 3 coming high and setting a screen on 1's defender. If the defenders do not switch, player 1 can drive in for the high-percentage shot. To insure that there will not be defensive help from 2's man, player 2 must entertain his defender by first walking his man low, then high. If there is a switch, the roll will be available for 3 along with a smaller defender on him. This screen is signaled by player 1 with a closed fist or other visual key developed in practice. Note that 2 comes high for defensive balance. (Diagram 1-38)

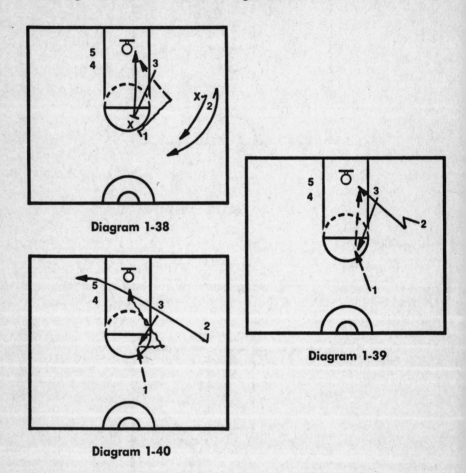

Diagram 1-38

Diagram 1-39

Diagram 1-40

Backdoor Series

This defensive pressure counter-move is used when 1 is having difficulty getting the ball to wing guard 2. If 2 senses a strong overplay by his man, which will occur after several successful moves by 2, he signals 1 by extending his left arm out at his side. Player 1 then closes his fist with his free hand, telling 3 to come high. Player 3 now comes high above the free-throw line with a hard jump-stop, receives the pass from 1, "shapes up" with a front pivot and looks for 2 who has executed a Z-cut to the basket. If 2 is covered, player 3 can drop-step and drive to the basket as 2 clears to the opposite side. (Diagrams 1-39 and 1-40)

> **COACHING POINT:** **The backdoor should only be used occasionally. Overuse of this maneuver decreases its effectiveness. Also, timing is very important in the execution of this play, and substantial practice time must be devoted to insure some measure of success with it. Your players should be instructed <u>never</u> to force this play. To do so usually results in an unwanted turnover instead of a layup.**

End-of-Period Offense

You should try to score whenever possible! Over the years I've witnessed many games where players are unaware of the amount of time left in the quarter, especially during the first half. The result is either no shot at all or a hurried attempt which I call a "hope shot."

Rotating into the Stack

If you have possession of the ball with about thirty seconds remaining in a period, your team should spread out to insure possession, then rotate into a double low-stack with the wing guards, players 2 and 5, behind the post men, players 3 and 4. With approximately 15 seconds remaining, the point guard should select the side where he feels the least amount of defensive pressure and should then initiate the attack.

The "Quick Popper"

If 1 dribbles right, player 2 taps 3 for a down-screen and pops out for the pass from 1. Player 2 can shoot, work one-on-one for the last-second shot or "jam-it" low to the big man for the power shot with a few seconds remaining, with the possibility of a second shot. If you are not successful, you will be reasonably sure your opponents won't be either.

You can see that the end-of-period offense is an option from the Basic Inside-Out Attack. When you drill on one, you are actually drilling on the other as well. This repetition insures sound execution and offensive proficiency, and that's a good reason to use similar options from different formations. (Diagram 1-41)

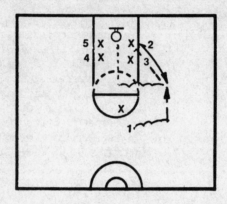

Diagram 1-41

Rebound Responsibilities

Strive to have one or both of your big men near the basket for the all-important second or third attempt at the basket. Getting the offensive rebound and scoring from it could be one of the key reasons for your overall success with these offensive attacks. The point guard, player 1, or wing guard, player 2, should always be back for balance to defend against your opponent's attempt at the transition basket. If 2 shoots, player 1 should stay back, and vice-versa. In addition, since the Basic Inside-Out Attack is initiated from a single stack alignment, you should make it a rule to have the up man in the stack responsible for the middle rebound. This leaves three offensive rebounders relatively close to the basket and a long rebounder in player 1 or 2. Many rebounds that cannot be directly controlled underneath can be tapped out, kept alive and in your possession, with designated player 1 or 2 staying back.

You should work extra hard on both offensive and defensive rebounding. Elimination drills should be used in practice to keep the players working for the rebound. Also, work on faking before releasing to the ball. This keeps the defenders, who are trying to block you out, off balance. In addition to blocking-out drills, teach your players to "roll-off" the men trying to block them out. This is executed by placing the inside arm and leg between the defender and the basket after the attempted block-out, then pivoting on the inside foot and ending up in a side-by-side position with the defender. This gives your players an equal opportunity to rebound and maintain possession of the ball.

Drills for the
Basic Inside-Out Attack

Three of the most important drills necessary for the development of The Basic Inside-Out Attack are: the pick-and-roll, hitting the stack and the baseline series. Constant drilling on these maneuvers can increase your offensive efficiency tremendously.

Pick and Roll

Diagram 1-42 illustrates the pick-and-roll drill. Player 1 dribbles the ball towards player 2, who uses a change-of-direction move to get rid of his man. Player 1 then hits 2 with the pass. Player 2 must set up his defender with a dribble-move or jab-step before he can use the pick set by player 3. It is important that player 2 use the pick set by 3 and not just free-lance. Player 3 positions himself with a wide base and allows the defender at least one step (legal screen). As soon as 2 has a step on the defender, player 3 opens and rolls to the ball, looking for a pass from 2. The lob and bounce passes should be used in this drill. Rotations: Player 1 goes to the end of line 3, player 3 moves to the end of line 2 and player 2 goes to the end of line 1. Designate a defender each day, so that all the players learn to fight through picks.

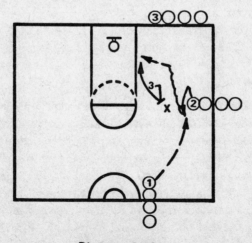

Diagram 1-42

Hitting the Stack

Diagram 1-43 illustrates the drill used to hit the stack. The first player in line 2 and the first player in line 3 step out and set up in tandem. As soon as player 1 dribbles to the stack side, player 3 taps 2, signaling him to screen 3's man. Player 3 pops out and up, and after receiving the pass, assumes the triple-threat position. Have player 3 either shoot or "jam" the ball low. You can alternate the shot selection or designate the shot for each day you use this drill.

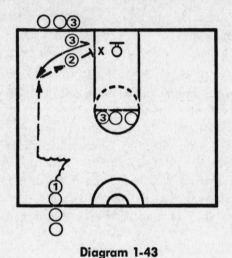

Diagram 1-43

You cannot overemphasize the screening technique used in this maneuver. Solid screens are the backbone for getting off high-percentage shots. Rotation: Player 1 goes to the end of line 3, player 3 goes to the end of line 2 and player 2 retires to the end of line 1.

Baseline Series

The drill for getting into the baseline is shown in Diagram 1-44. Player 2, using a change-of-direction move, cuts along the baseline, hooks player 3 as he goes by and receives a pass from player 1. Player 2 can either shoot or "jam" the ball low to 3 for a close-in power shot. Note that this is the same maneuver used when 2 passes back to 1 and cuts under the defense described earlier in this chapter. Player 2 must hook the player screening for him so he pops out at the proper angle to receive the pass. Rotation: Player 3 moves to line 2, player 2 moves to line 1 and player 1 moves to the end of line 3.

These are not all of the drills used to break down offensive maneuvers, but they are the three major ones. After selecting the options that fit your personnel, you can devise drills to break down your other maneuvers to ensure sound execution. For example, the backdoor maneuver and having the low men "explode" to the ball are just two other maneuvers that can be broken down into drill form.

Diagram 1-44

2

A Clear-Out Series for Your Best Shooter

An Auxiliary Man-for-Man Attack

Very often, the coach with a talented player faces the problem of where to play him. In many cases, he is the best shooter, ball handler and rebounder. Do you want him to bring the ball up-court to start the attack, then become a part of it; do you want him to set up close to the basket; or do you want him to be the heart of the first and second options?

45

Relationship to the
Inside-Out Attack

Although the Clear-Out Series is somewhat of a new pattern, it is closely related to the basic Inside-Out Attack and is easy to teach. The ease with which your players can execute the Clear-Out Series is due to the fact that the options remain very similar regardless of what attacking formation is used. This eliminates confusion on the part of the players. If you do not have an extremely talented player on your team, this auxiliary attack is probably unnecessary.

As every basketball coach knows, basketball preparation time is at a premium, and any ingredient that can be implemented quickly into the offensive or defensive arsenal is probably worth the effort. The ease with which you can implement the Clear-Out Series is a definite point in its favor if you have the personnel to accommodate its requirements.

Diagram 2-1 illustrates the basic Inside-Out alignment discussed in Chapter 1. In Diagram 2-2 the simple move of stacking your side post, player 3, with 4 and 5 has isolated 2, your best shooter, on the right side with plenty of operating room. How well 2 reads his defender will determine what move he will make. He decides to shoot, drive or pass back to 1 to start the continuity. Like the rule-oriented motion offense (where passing, screening, cutting and reading the defense are musts) it is imperative that 2 be able to read his defender before making his move. To make this series and other attacks work more effectively, drill your players daily on various one-on-one moves.

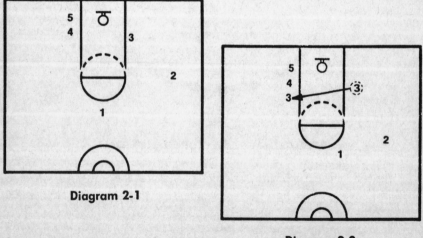

Diagram 2-1

Diagram 2-2

Take Advantage of a Weak Defense

You can go right into your Clear-Out Series if you discover that your opponent has a weak defensive set against your best offensive player. However, there are several schools of thought here. Some coaches feel it is best to hold down an explosive offensive player with various overplays and "stunting" maneuvers. Others concede his point production and concentrate on holding down the other four players. Some coaches will deploy a box-and-one or some other combination defense against your team. These should have little effect on your execution, because the triple-stack formation distorts any defense. Let's take a look at Diagram 2-3, where a box-and-one is used against the Clear-Out Series. As you can see, the one-guard front and triple stack has placed a definite disadvantage on the defense. Although 2 is covered, player 1 is not being defended at all, allowing penetration. Player X5 has to cover three men at once, and X4 is wasted. By "spotting-up" into the gaps of the box, you can get high-percentage shots. After hitting several of those, you may force the defense into a straight-man defense. Forcing the defense into a man-for-man situation will allow your best shooter the opportunity to work one-on-one. The box-and-one is also a poor rebounding defense against the second and third shots.

Once your opponents are in their man-for-man coverage, instruct your point guard to get the ball to 2 and let him work his man until the opposition makes an adjustment.

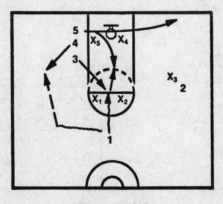

Diagram 2-3

Diagram 2-4 illustrates 2 dipping and coming back to receive a pass from 1. After receiving this pass, player 2 must face the basket where he is in the triple-threat position. He can shoot, drive or pass.

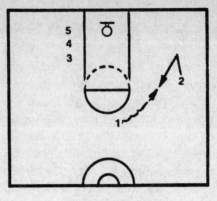

Diagram 2-4

As shown in Diagram 2-5, player 2 fakes left and takes his man across the baseline for the power layup or the short jumper.

If any weakside help arrives, as shown in Diagram 2-6 with X5 coming over, player 2 can pass off to 5 and you get an easy two points.

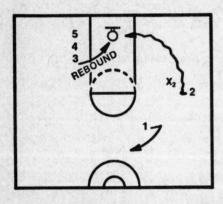

Diagram 2-5

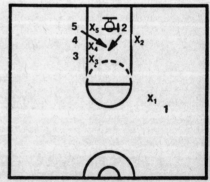

Diagram 2-6

Relieve Guard Pressure

Two-Man Pick-and-Roll

If your point guard is pressured, send 2 up to execute a pick-and-roll, placing 1's smaller man on 2's back and allowing 2 an open alley to the basket. (Diagram 2-7)

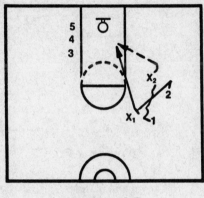

Diagram 2-7

Posting Low

After executing the pick-and-roll with the point guard, player 1, if 2 cannot receive a pass, he posts his smaller man low as shown in Diagram 2-8. Player 2 is now in the advantageous position of being in the low-post area and having a smaller defender on his back. He can now work his man in close for the high-percentage shot and many times for the three-point play.

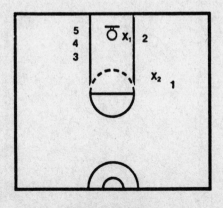

Diagram 2-8

Another way you can post 2's man is to have 2 drive his man into the free-throw lane, buttonhook and receive a "power pass" from the point guard, player 1. After reading the defense, player 2 can elect to get off a short jumper or take a quick dribble and power layup. (Diagram 2-9)

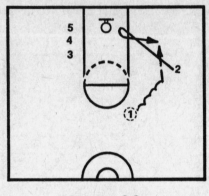

Diagram 2-9

This maneuver is triggered when 2 sees 1 dribbling toward him. This is his signal to clear out the right side, allowing the point guard an opportunity to drive all the way or providing him with an excellent passing angle to 2 as he buttonhooks and comes back toward the ball. If 1 clearly has his man beat, he will continue in for the layup, and 2 has the option of clearing to the right corner or continuing behind the triple stack. In the latter case, player 3 moves out for defensive floor balance. (Diagram 2-10)

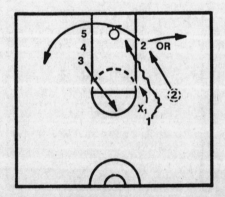

Diagram 2-10

Backdoor

The backdoor cut is certainly not new, but it is still an effective counter to defensive overplay. If your best shooter feels that he is being played too closely and his man is creating passing problems for your point guard, he should give the point man a hand signal indicating that he wants to fake coming to the ball and wants to go "backdoor."

Diagram 2-11 illustrates a backdoor cut in the Clear-Out Series. As 1 dribbles toward 2, player 2 senses X_2's overplay and signals by extending his left arm out about thigh high. This simple move further stimulates the defender's overaggressiveness while increasing his vulnerability to the reverse-cut to the basket.

As soon as 2 reverses his direction and has his man on his back, 1 executes a bounce pass as 2 clears into the open lane. The bounce pass, being a slower pass, is much easier to handle by a fast-moving target.

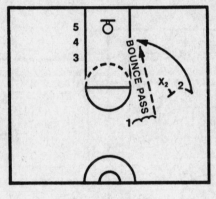

Diagram 2-11

Continuity Pattern

Clear-Out

Your first option is for the point guard 1 to look and pass to 2, who must dip and come back to receive 1's pass. It is necessary for the defender to think that there is the possibility that 2 may cut hard for the basket. It is much easier for 2 to get open with this "dipping" or change-of-direction move. (Diagram 2-12)

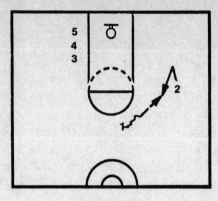

Diagram 2-12

Upon receipt of this pass, player 2 can shoot, drive to the basket or work one-on-one as close to the basket as possible before he decides to pass back to 1, who now slides closer to the original spot held by 2. (Diagram 2-13)

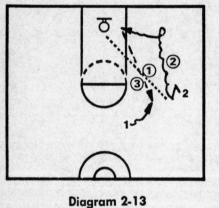

Diagram 2-13

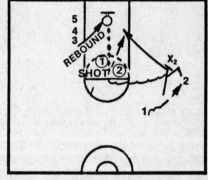

Diagram 2-14

As a variation to this, player 1 will pick 2's man after the first pass, allowing 2 to come over the top for the quick jumper or to execute the pick-and-roll. (Diagram 2-14)

COACHING POINT: The up man on the stack side has middle rebound responsibilities. As already mentioned, if either 2 or 1 beats his man, this forces a defensive switch, leaving either 4 or 5 open for an easy layup.

Scissor

In Diagram 2-15, 1 fills the spot vacated by 2 as 2 maneuvers for a shot. If 2 is stopped, he passes back to 1 and stays low, which keys the next option.

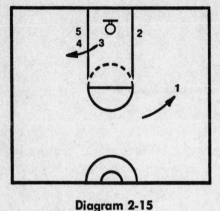

Diagram 2-15

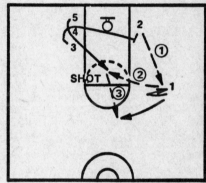

Diagram 2-16

Diagram 2-16 shows the next move. Player 1, after receiving a return pass from 2, looks for 5, who has scissored off 4 in combination with 3 for a quick pass and jump-shot in the lane. Player 3 is your reserve post and is really a decoy in this sequence. But, if he is open, your players should not hesitate to get him the ball for the close-in shot.

Players 2 and 3 are stacked low, waiting for 5 if he cannot shoot. If 5 is unable to shoot, he must quickly pass back to 1, who has moved closer to the top of the key.

In Diagram 2-17, player 4 sees that 5 can not shoot, passes back to the point guard, player 1, and moves quickly to a high post at the free-throw line extended. He should now look for a pass from 1 and take his shot or move one-on-one to the basket. At this point, player 4 has had his side cleared so that he can turn on his one-on-one game.

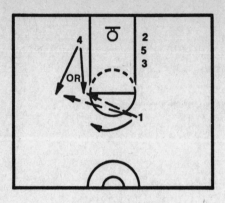

Diagram 2-17

If 4 cannot make his move, players 3 and 2 scissor off 5, as illustrated in Diagram 2-18. Player 3 cuts low along the baseline, and 2, whom you want to take the shot, is coming high toward the ball.

> **COACHING POINT:**   In the event that 2 is not open for the shot, he <u>must</u> continue to his right, staying <u>well away</u> from the free-throw lane. He is now preparing for another cut and if he is too close to the free-throw lane, the players setting his screen may be caught for a three-second violation.

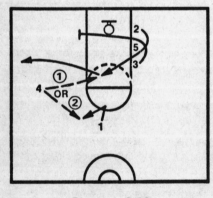

Diagram 2-18

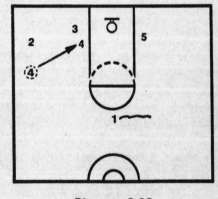

Diagram 2-19

Meanwhile, Player 4 has returned the ball to the point guard, player 1, and has set a double-screen with 3. (Diagram 2-19)

Reverse Action

The last sequence to this Clear-Out Series is illustrated in Diagram 2-20, with 5 popping out and receiving a pass from 1. Player 5 now has the same options that 2 had in Diagram 2-12. He can shoot or go one-on-one.

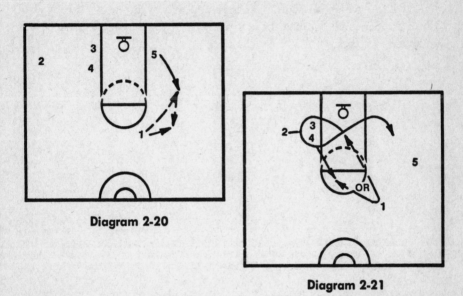

Diagram 2-20

Diagram 2-21

If neither of these options is available to him, he returns the ball to 1, who quickly looks for 2, who is running his man into the double-screen provided by 3 and 4. Player 2 has the option of going high or low for a high-percentage shot. (Diagram 2-21)

After passing back to 1, player 5 moves along the baseline to his original spot, and with 2 moving to his left, you are now back in your original set.

COACHING POINT: After 2 runs his man into the double screen, the up man, player 4, should pivot and "explode" to the ball for a possible pass if 2 is not open. (Diagram 2-21) Remember, the up man on the stack has middle rebound responsibilities unless he is shooting. The low man on the stack must slide across the lane and assume rebound responsibilities on that side. All sound offenses must provide offensive rebounding!

The success of this auxiliary attack is mainly the result of the fact that it is quite similar to the basic Inside-Out Attack. It is easy to execute, and because fewer people are handling the ball, there are fewer turnovers.

The Clear-Out Series succeeds in allowing your best shooter to take advantage of a weak defender, to play his one-on-one game for extended periods of time and to obtain the high-percentage shot.

If you have an outstanding player you may want to use this type of Clear-Out Series as your man-for-man attack. Or, you may want to install it as an auxiliary attack.

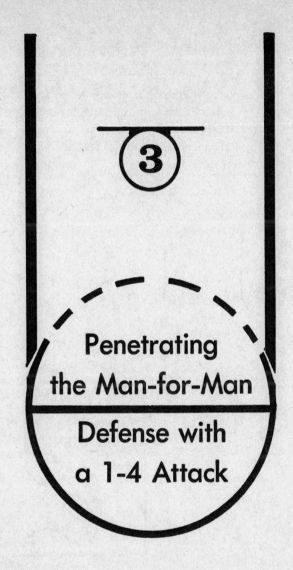

3

Penetrating the Man-for-Man Defense with a 1-4 Attack

The 1-4 alignment pulls your opponent's big men away from the basket, providing your post men and wing guards with operating room to go one-on-one to the basket.

This formation provides the point man with four entry passes. He can pass to either post man, player 3 or 4, or to either wing guard, player 2 or 5. These entries are in the high-percentage shooting area and create vulnerability within the defense. There is little weakside defensive help against this formation and its options. The defense is hurt by the quick shot, backdoor maneuvers and the clear-outs.

Alignment

The 1-4 alignment is operable from either a high or medium post. By changing the starting point, you keep the defense off balance. If the defense elects to overplay, you should move high, opening the backdoor options. If they play loose, you should set up low and take the short jump-shots available.

Diagrams 3-1 and 3-2 illustrate personnel placement. In Diagram 3-1, the high-post 1-4 is shown and in Diagram 3-2 the medium-post 1-4 is illustrated.

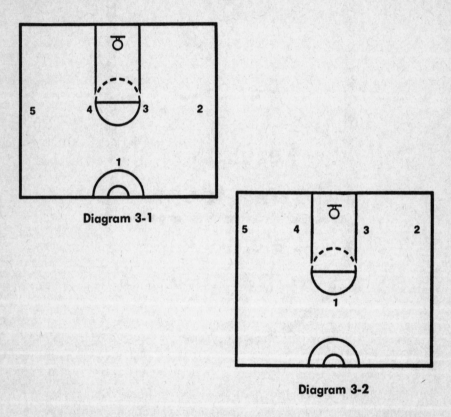

Diagram 3-1

Diagram 3-2

When using either formation, the big men must be cautioned not to set up on the lines of the free-throw lane. This oversight can result in a three-second violation.

The post men should be instructed to straddle the key-hole circle, one step above the free-throw line in the high 1-4 formation, and they should also be told to stay one step away from the free-throw lane in the medium-post 1-4.

This chapter illustrates play from the high-post 1-4 alignment.

Establishing a Strongside

The strongside is established as soon as player 1 moves to either side of an imaginary line dividing the full court. Until the point guard decides which side to attack, the defense is at a disadvantage. If they play tight and overplay either the wing or the post, they are inviting the backdoor. When they've been burned by the backdoor, they begin to play loose, allowing the short jump shot. Both of these quick hitters are high-percentage offensive moves and you should be ready to take whatever the defense is willing to give you.

In Diagram 3-3, the point man can get the ball to the wing guard, player 2, who gets rid of his man by dipping to the basket and coming back toward the ball. Player 2 should present a target with his left hand to remind player 1 to pass away from the defensive man.

Upon receipt of the ball, player 2 turns to face the basket and assumes the triple-threat position. If his man plays him loose, then 2 should shoot; if the defense elects to play player 2 head-to-head, player 2 can work his man one-on-one for the close-in shot.

NOTE: **Player 1 should fill the vacated area left by 2's penetration. In case the ball has to be reversed (remember, these options work against zone defenses),
player 1 is in position to do so. (Diagram 3-4)**

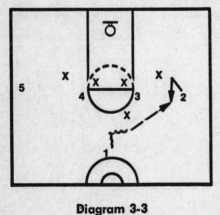

Diagram 3-3

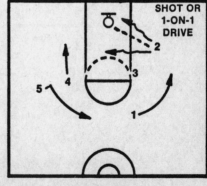

Diagram 3-4

Executing the Pick-and-Roll
(Coming-over-the Top)

If player 2 decides not to shoot or take his man low, he teams with player 3, who is on the strongside high post, and executes a pick-and-roll maneuver by coming high and going over-the-top. This is the same option and results in the same continuity that is in the Basic Inside-Out Attack. (Diagram 3-5)

Getting into the Baseline Series

Meanwhile, the high post, player 4, seeing the ball passed to player 2, assumes his offensive or baseline series position in the weakside low post. (Diagram 3-5)

Player 5, the weakside wing guard, moves toward the spot vacated by player 1, in anticipation of reversal of the ball and a pass to player 2 who can get into the baseline series by rubbing his man off a screen set by 4 down low. (Diagram 3-5)

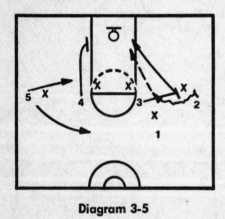

Diagram 3-5

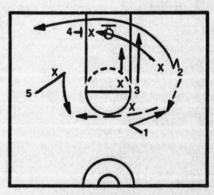

Diagram 3-6

Reversing to the Weakside

If player 2 cannot execute any of the aforementioned options, he can pass the ball back to player 1, who reverses the ball to 5, who looks for 2 rubbing off 4 or for 4 in low for the close-in power move. (Diagram 3-6)

COACHING POINT: It is important to remind your players to get rid of their defenders by using a change-of-direction move to get open before moving to the ball. This is especially important if the defense is over-playing the passing lanes.

Diagram 3-7, shows the wing guard, player 5, with the ball, looking for 2 or 4, who are in the baseline series alignment.

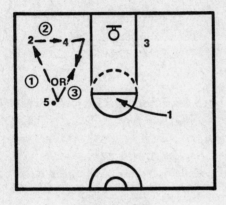

Diagram 3-7

If player 2 successfully rubs his man off 4, he should be open for the baseline jumper. If player 4 is being played from behind by his defender, 2 can "jam" the ball in deep, allowing 4 to maneuver for the close-in power shot. Player 5 also has the option of hitting player 4 directly if 4 reads his defender and comes back for the ball. (Diagram 3-7.)

If player 2 shoots from the corner, the rebound triangle is formed with players 4, 3 and 1. Player 5 stays back for balance. If player 4 shoots, players 2, 3 and 1 have rebound responsibilities, with 5 staying back.

Two other successful options that can be used from this point are the flash-cut by 3 and a rear screen set by 3 for player 1.

Flash-Cut

In Diagram 3-8, player 4, who has the ball and is facing the basket, looks for player 3, the other post man, who puts a change-of-direction move on his man, flashes across the lane towards the ball and looks for a pass from 4. This is a good strong maneuver, especially if the 3 man is left-handed. He is in excellent position for the layup, jump hook or short jump-shot.

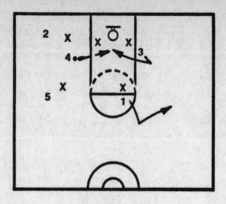

Diagram 3-8
Flash cut by 3

Rear Screen

Another effective move from this set involves having player 3 fake the flash and go up and set a rear screen on 1's defender. This play is signaled by the point guard, player 1, who must be certain that he has the advantage in this case. Normally, you should not remove a big man from the low post unless you feel he can be successful in executing this rear screen. It is, however, an excellent move if properly executed. (Diagram 3-9)

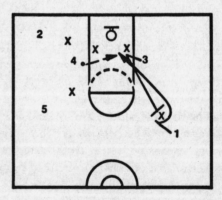

Diagram 3-9
Rear Screen for 1

Post Roll-and-Exchange

If player 4 cannot perform his options, he passes back to player 5 or 2, depending on who is open, and executes the post roll-and-exchange maneuver with player 3. Player 4, after passing, clears across the lane and 3 replaces him by moving high, rolling low to the ball and then looking for a pass from either 2 or 5. (Diagram 3-10) The mechanics of this move and the screening mechanics in the baseline series are the same as those explained in Chapter 1.

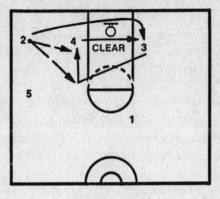

Diagram 3-10

Reversing to the Weakside. In Diagram 3-10, player 2 passes to 3 rolling low. If he cannot execute this option or create any original action himself, he passes back to 5, who in turn reverses the ball to player 1, who is stationed near the top of the key. Player 2, meanwhile, moves baseline, hooks his man off a screen set by player 4 and looks for a pass from point guard 1. (Diagram 3-11)

Diagram 3-11

Player 1, of course, can hit 4 deep, as 5 was able to in the baseline series.

If 2 shoots, players 3, 4 and 5 have rebound responsibilities with 1 back for floor balance. Player 2 has the same options on this side of the floor as he had in the baseline series. Player 2 can "jam" the ball in low to 4 if he has his man on his back.

In Diagram 3-11, note the ideal rebounding triangle set up with players 3, 4 and 5. This superior offensive rebounding positioning can be a major factor affecting your overall success.

Strongside Post Roll-and-Exchange. If 2 cannot hit 4, player 4 clears out and 3 comes high and rolls low, anticipating a pass from 2. In these inside big-man maneuvers, your players should be instructed to use their bodies, make themselves "big" and want the ball. They use footwork and head and shoulder fakes to beat their defenders to the desired spots. You don't want any of your flash-cuts blocked by the defense. This clear-out maneuver between players 3 and 4 places the players into a medium 1-4, and the entire series can start again, depending on whether player 2 passes back to 1 or not. Diagram 3-12 illustrates this exchange and player 2 passing back out front to the point guard. The point guard should "read" the defense and choose an entry from which the pattern phase can continue.

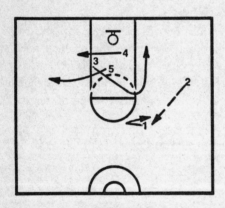

Diagram 3-12

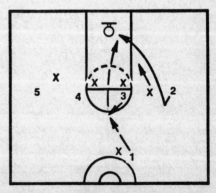

Diagram 3-13

Getting into the Baseline Series
from the High Post

Diagram 3-13 illustrates player 1 making a semi-lob pass to the strongside high post, player 3. Player 3 immediately pivots, faces the basket and looks for the wing guard, player 2, cutting to the goal on a backdoor maneuver. Player 2 must fake high, then cut hard for the goal. If 2 is open, player 3 should get him the ball with a semi-lob pass in the layup position. That is, player 2 should receive the pass with a jump stop and power the ball up off the board.

> NOTE: The side to which the entry pass is made establishes the strongside. The weakside post player then slides down, setting the screen for the Baseline Series.

If 2 is not open, he continues baseline and rubs his man off the weakside post, player 4, who moved down the free-throw lane. Player 1 moves the ball quickly to player 5, who in turn has all of the previously mentioned baseline series options. He can now pass the ball to 2 or 4 or wait for the post roll-and-exchange. Player 3 must wait to see what develops before assuming his rebound responsibilities. (Diagram 3-14)

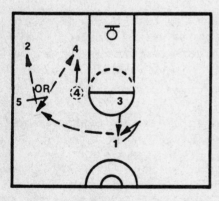

Diagram 3-14

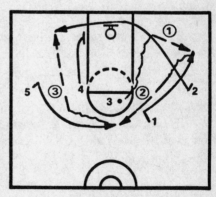

Diagram 3-15

If 3 did not return the ball to player 1 as shown in Diagram 3-13, it should be noted that after 2 clears out, the entire right side is open for 3 to go one-on-one with his man. Diagram 3-15 shows 3 doing just that. If he is stopped, he can pass to player 1, who has filled for 2, player 1 can pass to 5, who has filled for player 1, and player 5 can look for the baseline series options with players 2 and 4. This constant motion and passing of the ball keeps the defense a step or two behind.

Guard Clear

From the high 1-4 series you can also involve the point guard by using a clear-out maneuver by either wing guard. As soon as player 1 establishes a strongside and he wants to execute this clearing maneuver, he does so by calling out, "Clear." This tells the strongside wing guard to clear out and allow the point guard operating room. When the wing guard does clear out, he assumes the baseline series position with the weakside post man.

Let's take a look at this maneuver in Diagram 3-16. Player 1 establishes the strongside to his right and signals "clear", chasing 2 opposite and into his baseline set with post man 4. Player 3, now sets a high pick on 1's defender allowing 1 to dribble and rub his man off the pick.

If 1 cannot beat his man, or if there is a switch on defense, he and player 3 can attempt to execute the pick-and-roll option, which is also illustrated in Diagram 3-16.

Player 5, meanwhile, replaces 1 at the top of the key in case the ball has to be reversed. If the ball is reversed, as shown in Diagram 3-17, player 5 dribbles to his left and hits 2 "popping" out from a screen set by 4. You are then in the baseline series again, to be followed by the post roll-and-exchange.

Backdoor Series

The backdoor series is illustrated in Diagram 3-18. Player 1 passes a semi-lob pass to player 3. Instead of 2 cutting backdoor as in the clear-out options, we have the weakside post and weakside guard team up. After 3 receives the pass from 1, the weakside post, player 4, moves down the lane and then comes back, setting a rear screen on 5's man.

The rear screen set on the weakside, catches the defense napping, and you can usually obtain the high-percentage shot and sometimes even get the three-point play.

Rebound Responsibilities

All of the options and special situations can be mirrored on the opposite side of the court in all of the attacks; rebounding is no exception. You should have both of your big men near the basket on all rebound assignments, with the weakside guard taking the middle. Player 1 has ½-man responsibility on long rebounds if he is not shooting; if he does shoot, the strongside wing guard must stay back for defensive floor balance.

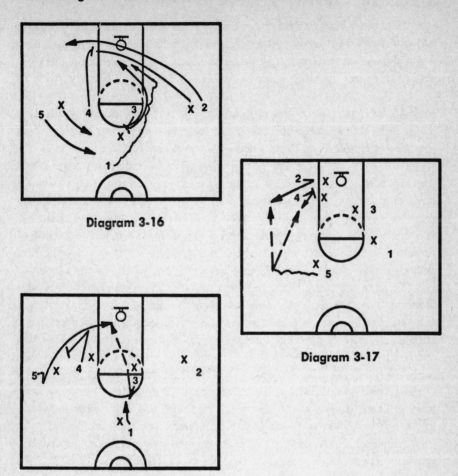

Diagram 3-16

Diagram 3-17

Diagram 3-18

Fundamental Factors for Offensive Rebounding

Offensive rebounding can contribute greatly to your overall success. By design, having your big men close to the basket will ensure an opportunity at the second and third shots. Even if they can't secure a rebound, they may be able to tip the ball out and your team can gain another possession.

Positioning is the most important factor in offensive rebounding (i.e., anticipating where the ball will come off the board or rim and moving to that spot), and there are three fundamental factors that can put you in the most advantageous position.

First, your players must know their teammates' shooting habits. It is of prime importance that each player shoot when he is within *his* scoring range. Through practiced execution of your offense in daily practice, your players will get the right feel, learning when and where each man will be most likely to shoot.

About 75 percent of missed shots fall to the weakside. Since our offense is designed for strong inside and baseline maneuvers, our players head for those appropriate rebound positions when a shot is taken.

Bank shots, however, are usually short when missed and come off either the front of the rim or to the side the shot was taken from. It is, therefore, important that your players know when a bank shot will be taken so that they can anticipate and beat their defenders to the inside rebound position.

Second, your players should use fakes to keep their defenders occupied. If the defender is overly concerned about a player's movements, he won't have enough time to locate the ball, thus lessening his chance for the rebound.

Third, teach your players the use of the roll-off in securing the offensive rebound. You should use this maneuver when the defender has you pretty well blocked out. The roll-off is used when your man is beside his defender on the strongside. If the shot is taken from the right side, he should place his left arm and left leg inside the defender's mid-section and right leg. He should then pivot on his left leg and complete a 360-degree turn. This will place the offensive man in a side-by-side position with the defender, but the *offensive* man will have the weakside rebounding position, and that's what he wants. If the offensive man is on the left side, reverse the technique.

Above all, convince your players that if they want to score, they have to rebound. They should understand that if they get the offensive board, they'll probably have the next offensive maneuver.

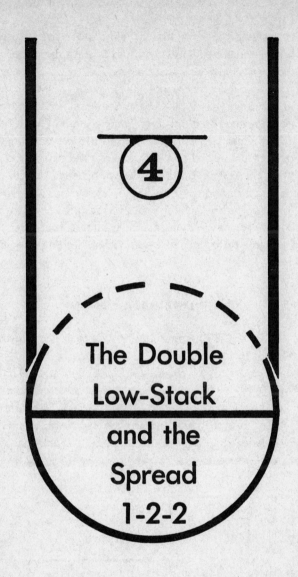

4

The Double Low-Stack and the Spread 1-2-2

Two other formations that you can use against both the man-for-man and zone defense are the Double Low-Stack and the Spread 1-2-2. Each of these offenses has its advantages and adaptabilities to the defenses you face. By taking advantage of your strengths and the defense's weaknesses, you can determine whether you want to develop an inside power game with the stack or open the key, spread the defense out and allow for more one-on-one penetration with the 1-2-2 attack.

Remember, as with the other attacks, while the initial offensive sets are different, the basic options are identical with only slight modifications to take advantage of the defensive weaknesses present.

Both attacks allow for penetration by the point guard. However, the Double Low-Stack allows you to take advantage of one or two strong inside players and at least one good medium-range jump-shooter. On the other hand, the Spread 1-2-2 provides for penetration by all five players plus the strong inside game. If you have several players who are good penetrators and good one-on-one players the Spread 1-2-2 may prove beneficial to you.

Also, the spread formation of the 1-2-2 can aid a team that is smaller than its opponents, because the big men can be moved away from the goal area. The 1-2-2 is also a popular formation to use as a delay offense, because the defense is spread and can't double-team any one player without leaving an offensive man wide open to receive the ball.

Getting into the Stack

Diagrams 4-1 and 4-2 illustrate how easy it is to get into the Double Low-Stack formation from the Basic Inside-Out set.

Diagram 4-1 shows the Basic Inside-Out formation, and in Diagram 4-2, the simple move of placing the wing guard, player 2, behind the post man, player 3, will put you into the Double Low-Stack set. The entire offensive series can be executed from the stack, because the responsibilities of the players doesn't change. This is the beauty of using multiple formations. While the sets vary in physical structure, the players' responsibilities do not.

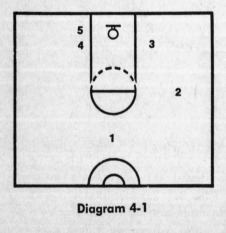

Diagram 4-1

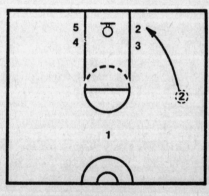

Diagram 4-2

Advantages of the Double Low-Stack

- Can be used as a quick-shot or continuity offense.
- Can be used against man-for-man and zone defenses.
- Takes advantage of any defensive weaknesses.
- Provides high-percentage scoring opportunities.
- Keeps your big men close to the basket whether they are post players, forwards or a post-forward combination.
- Allows for penetration by the point guard.
- Allows you to get the ball to your best shooters with a minimum of passes.
- Fewer people handle the ball; thus, fewer turnovers.
- Provides for excellent offensive rebounding.
- The one-guard set is harder to double-team.
- Because most teams practice defense against the more conventional offenses (2-1-2, 1-3-1, and the 1-2-2), the stack poses defensive problems.
- It is not a physically tiring offense.
- The offense can be mirrored from either side.

Disadvantages of the Double Low-Stack

- Timing is vital in this attack. If the players do not react to the point guards' keys, the defense can adjust and nullify any surprise element on the part of the offense.
- Because there is only one guard and the other four players are close to the basket, this attack is susceptible to the fast break.
- This offense should not be used for an entire game. The fast break, an auxiliary offense and a trapping defense that provides scoring opportunities will make the stack much more effective.
- Without off-the-ball player movement, there will be weakside defensive help.

Offensive Keys

The importance of the point guard, player 1, as a play-maker in the stack offense cannot be overemphasized. He has to have the ability to: beat pressure, go one-on-one with his man, be an outside scoring threat as well as an excellent passer and be an excellent defensive player in stopping the opposition's transition baskets.

Players 2 and 5 are the wing guards, and they have to be good medium-range shooters, especially player 2, because the offense usually starts to his side and he is involved in the baseline series more than player 5. They have to be adequate rebounders and good passers in working the two-man games with the post players, players 3 and 4.

The posts, players 3 and 4, should be aggresive offensive players with the ability to play with their backs to the basket. Player 3 should be the better offensive player of the two. Both players should be strong one-on-one players in close, with the ability to use the hook shot, reverse-pivot and drop-step moves.

Establishing a Strongside

The defense usually dictates what side of the court to attack. However, the right side is normally the strongside, the left being the weakside. As with your other attacks, the offense will be illustrated as being initiated from the strongside.

The offensive players, all facing the ball handler and as tight together as possible, should wait until the point guard has taken at least two steps in their direction before getting into motion. The reason for this is that the point guard may use a reverse dribble on his man and elect to attack the other side.

Screening by the Post Man. Assuming that player 1 has chosen to attack the right side and that player 2 sees that, player 2 will tap player 3 signaling him to set a screen, which frees 2 for the quick jumper. (Diagram 4-3) This screen is executed in a 135-degree turn by player 3 as he pivots on his *outside* foot (left), swings his inside foot around as if stepping backward and faces player 3's defensive man. Player 2, after tapping 3, fakes into the lane then quickly pops out on a 45-degree angle, hooking his teammate as he goes by. This hooking or rubbing shoulders with 3 assures 2 that he will lose his man long enough to receive the pass from the point guard. As soon as the hooking maneuver is complete, player 3 completes a 360-degree turn on his left foot as he swings his right leg around, and, while facing the ball again, anticipates a pass from player 1. (This maneuver was previously explained and illustrated in Chapter 1, Diagrams 1-16 and 1-17.)

> **NOTE:** **If there is a defensive switch, player 3, after screen-ing and coming back to the ball, is usually open for a shot.**

If the wing guard, player 2, receives the pass, he should immediately assume the triple-threat position. He can shoot or "jam" the ball in low to 3. If 3's defender is on his back, he can execute a pick-and-roll with 3 or he can return the ball to the point guard and clear to the other side.

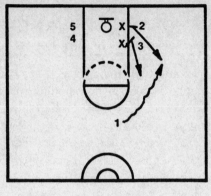

Diagram 4-3

When using the Double Low-Stack, your opponents may defense with four players in the free-throw lane. This would allow you to execute quite easily. However, the more defensive-minded coaches defense the stack by placing one player in front of the stack and one player in the lane. The up player is responsible for the pop-out maneuver, while the back man defends the post. Usually, this creates a mismatch in your favor, but if the players are of nearly equal size, you should flash the post player 3, high and run a backdoor with 2. (Diagram 4-4) Other options from this flash are available. One is illustrated in Diagram 4-5. Player 3 can take the ball to the goal, or a splitting maneuver with players 5 and 1 can be performed.

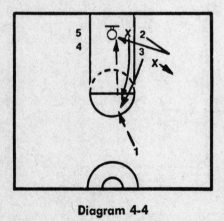

Diagram 4-4

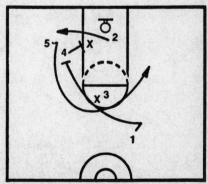

Diagram 4-5

"Jamming-It" to the Low Post

Assume that player 2 has just received the entry pass from the point guard. From the triple-threat position, player 2 can dribble, pass or shoot. Player 2 should shoot if he is open, but you should have him work with player 3, who is set up in the low post, which is a high-percentage area.

If 3's defender plays him on the high side, player 2 should pass the ball toward the baseline or *away* from the defense. Upon receipt of the ball with X3 playing on 3's outside hip, player 3 should make a quick *drop-step* move and power the ball up to the goal. (Diagram 4-6)

The drop-step move is executed by player 3 when he takes a long step with his left leg, and while turning, he swings his right leg around and shoots the power layup by going *up-and-in* to his defender. Some players feel they have to take a dribble before executing the drop-step. Either way is acceptable, as long as the move is executed quickly and the defender is closed out completely. Players 4 and 5 should make some positive movement to keep their defenders occupied and nullify any weakside defensive help.

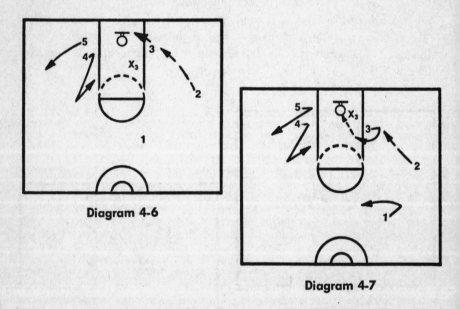

Diagram 4-6

Diagram 4-7

In Diagram 4-7, the defense is denying the ball to 3 from the baseline. Again, player 2 must pass away from X3. This time, player 3 fakes a move toward the baseline, using a quick half-step with his left leg. While showing X3 the ball, he reverse pivots on his right foot and completes the turn-around jump-shot. Players 4 and 5 again entertain their defenders by making purposeful movements.

Pick-and-Roll

If none of player 2's options are available or if he cannot "jam" the ball in deep to player 3, he can maintain his dribble and have 3 set a high or low pick for him. (Diagram 4-8)

The pick should be set on the left side of X₂ so that on his roll, player 3 can use the baseline area, which is free of defensive help. A defense that sags in the lane could stop this maneuver with weakside help if 3 is looking for the lob in the lane.

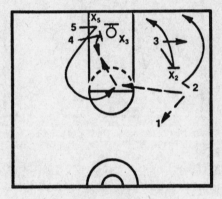

Diagram 4-8

Weakside Cut Over-the-Top

There are many scoring opportunities for players 2 and 3 on just one entry pass from player 1. However, if none of these options are open and if 2 quickly passes back to 1, player 5, using a change-of-direction move on his man and a screen by 4, comes over the top of the screen looking for the jumper in the lane. He should only come as high as necessary to receive this pass from 1. He could also take the pass from player 2 directly. (Diagram 4-8) To keep the defense honest, player 5 can fake coming up and sneak into the lane for a layup if his man tries to cut off his come-around move.

After player 4 screens 5's defender, he should quickly open to the ball. If he's open, 5 dumps the ball to him for the close-in power shot. (Diagram 4-8) 5 must quickly get out of the lane by moving to his left to avoid a three-second violation.

Getting into the Baseline Series

Meanwhile, player 2 moves along the baseline and is ready to team up with player 4 in the baseline series. Player 5 stacks with 3 on the left. Even if 1 is unable to reverse the ball to player 2 and hits 5, the whole aforementioned sequence could be executed with players 3 and 5.

Diagram 4-9 illustrates player 1 looking to hit either player 2 or 4 in the baseline series.

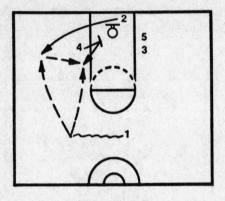

Diagram 4-9

Upon receipt of the pass, player 2 assumes the triple-threat position, looking to shoot, pass to 4 in the low post or penetrate through the lane looking for the high-percentage shot.

If player 4 receives the ball from either player 1 or 2, he should read his defenders position and quickly determine whether he wants to move baseline (drop-step maneuver) or reverse-pivot and take the turn-around-jumper in the lane. It is important that the post men realize that when they get the ball in close (the high-percentage area), we want them to be aggressive offensively. On any power moves in close, instruct your players to go up and in toward the goal, creating a possible three-point play situation. Many players simply go in to the defender and up to the basket, risking an offensive foul call. All of your baseline warm-up drills should incorporate the up-and-in thrust to the goal. This repetition keeps the players under control, and good body control is a must to good shooting.

Post Roll-and-Exchange

When player 4 realizes he will not get the ball in deep, he clears out to his left, allowing 3, who gets rid of his man, to come high. Then, while rolling low, he looks for the power move in close. (Diagram 4-10) If player 3 is successful in losing his man on his change-of-direction move, he should simply post himself in 4's previous post position and look for the power move. He only comes high if his man has not been shaken loose. Instruct your players to take their defenders away from their intended cuts. If we want the ball low, we'll move high and then low and vice-versa.

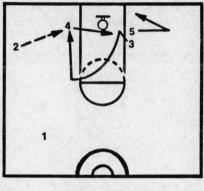

Diagram 4-10

Reversing to the Wing

If none of these options are available, player 2 returns the ball to player 1. Player 1 gets rid of his man and dribbles the ball to his right, looking for wing guard, player 5, who uses a screening maneuver by 3 and pops out to the area of the foul-line extended. Player 5 has all of the previously mentioned options with his low-post partner, player 4. (Diagram 4-11)

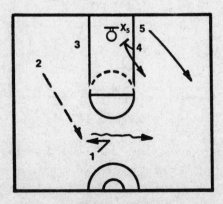

Diagram 4-11

Player 2, who is our best shooter, can also move to the ball by going baseline or coming over-the-top. In both cases (Diagram 4-12) he must use a change-of-direction move on his man to free himself. If 2 elects to go baseline, he can use a screen by 4 in moving to the corner. If he comes high, he can look to shoot or hit either 3 or 4, who pivot to the ball looking for the close-in power shot. (Diagram 4-13)

NOTE: **This positioning is very effective against zone defenses because there is a high-low situation, with the seams of the zone split and the overload principle against zone defenses with players 2, 4 and 5.**

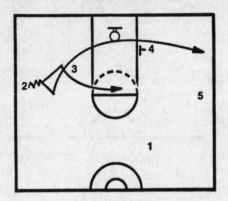

Diagram 4-12

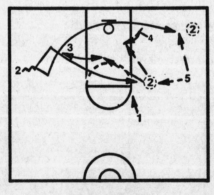

Diagram 4-13

If none of these options is available, player 5 can pass back to 1 and cut through, allowing for a post roll-and-exchange manuever and a complete resetting of the pattern. (Diagram 4-14)

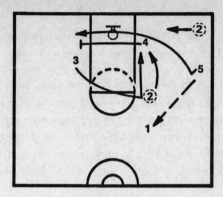

Diagram 4-14

Relieving Guard Pressure

Some teams try to disrupt offensive penetration by applying pressure tactics on player 1, either in the back court or as he crosses the mid-court stripe. This is countered by having either wing guard, player 2 or 5, bring the ball up court then assume his position, or he can exchange roles with player 1, filling the position for the "new" 1 man.

You can also flash the post, player 3, high to receive a pass if the point guard is pressured and either execute a give-and-go with 1 or a backdoor move with 2 from a rear screen set by 1 as he buttonhooks back. (Diagram 4-15) In either case, player 5 moves out to his wing position and looks for 3's pass and the baseline series.

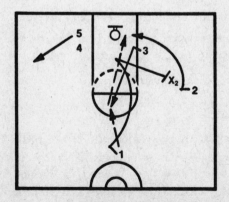

Diagram 4-15

Rebound Responsibilities

Your big men should be in close in their low-post positions for the offensive rebound unless they are logical shooters.

The up man on the stack side has middle rebound responsibilities to complete the triangle with the off wing guard assuming ½-man board play and player 1 back for defensive balance unless he is a shooter. If player 1 is shooting, the strongside wing guard must get back to slow up your opponent's transition game while the off wing guard takes the middle rebound area.

The Spread 1-2-2

Basic Formation

To complement your power game with the Stack Series, you can spread the defense by using a 1-2-2 formation. The basic formation for the 1-2-2 is illustrated in Diagram 4-16. The wing guards, players 5 and 2, take their positions at the foul-line extended and about 12' out. All of the players' responsibilities are the same as they are in the Basic Inside-Out alignment, the High 1-4, and the Double Low-Stack.

Open Key Advantages

The Spread 1-2-2, or open key formation, has some of the following advantages:

- It provides for numerous one-on-one and two-man game situations.
- It provides high-percentage shots for all the players.
- It provides good offensive rebounding positions.
- It adapts easily to a continuity or a free-lance game.
- It can be used against zone defenses.
- It is a good delay-game formation.

Strongside Entries

Unlike most 1-2-2 offensive alignments, you shouldn't mirror the attack against man-for-man defenses. If the point man initiates the offense with a pass to the wing guard, player 2, the strongside options follow (i.e., shoot, "jam-it" deep to 3, pick-and-roll, get into the baseline series). If the offense is started on the weakside, player 5 uses his weakside options (i.e., shoot, "jam-it" low to 4, post roll-and-exchange, look for 2 in the baseline series). Diagram 4-17 illustrates the strongside (right) and the weakside (left) set.

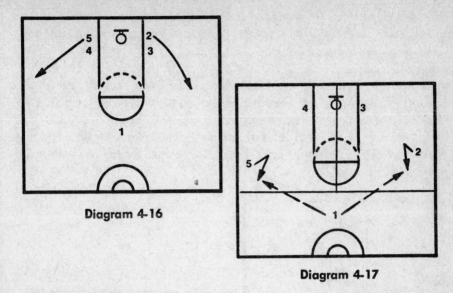

Diagram 4-16

Diagram 4-17

Guard to Wing Guard. In Diagrams 4-18 and 4-19, player 1 starts the attack with a pass to player 2, who uses a change-of-direction move on his man. Player 2 can shoot if he's open, "jam-it" deep to 3, execute a pick-and-roll with 3 or return the ball to 1 and get into the baseline series. Meanwhile, players 1, 4 and 5 entertain their defenders with purposeful movement.

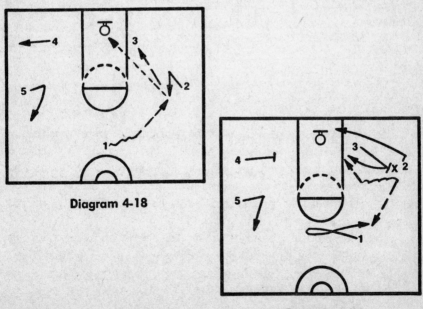

Diagram 4-18

Diagram 4-19

Guard to Post. If the wing guard, player 2, is being denied the ball, he is instructed to screen down for player 3 or cut to the basket and go into the baseline series. The post, player 3, seeing denial pressure on 2, flashes to the high post, calling for the ball from the point guard. Upon receipt of this pass, he pivots into the defensive man, looking for 2 on a backdoor cut to the goal. If 2 is covered, 3 can take his man one-on-one and reverse the ball to 5; player 5 can start the baseline series with 2 and 4. (Diagram 4-20) Another option we run when 2 clears out is to have player 1 and player 5 split the post if 3's options fail to develop. Player 4 may also be open for the power shot in close. (Diagram 4-21)

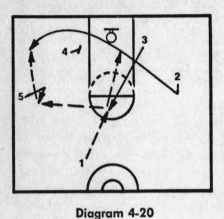

Diagram 4-20

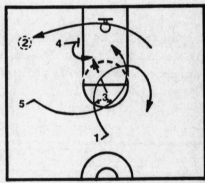

Diagram 4-21

Weakside Entries

Identical Keys. Player 1 initiates the weakside attack after establishing his weakside intent. The wing guard, player 5, loses his man with a change-of-direction move and receives the pass from point guard 1. Player 5 now has the identical options available to him as 2 had illustrated in Diagrams 4-18 and 4-19. However, the pass to 5 is really the key to execute the post roll-and-exchange with players 3 and 4. (Diagram 4-22).

If 5 cannot execute this option, he reverses the ball to 1, cuts under the defense and assumes the baseline series with player 4. 1 passes to 2 and 2 looks baseline for 5 or 3. These baseline screens have proven very effective against zone defenses as well as the man-for-man. (Diagram 4-23)

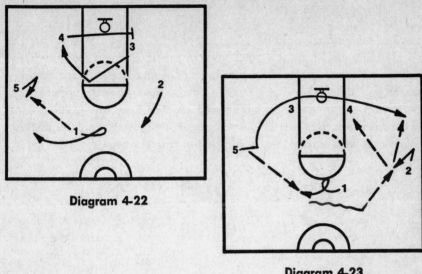

Diagram 4-22

Diagram 4-23

<u>Backdoor.</u> The backdoor option, illustrated in Diagram 4-20, with the wing guard, player 2, and the post, player 3, is also available to the other wing guard, player 5, and the other post, player 4, if the necessary conditions are present.

<u>Relieving Pressure.</u> If player 1 is having difficulty initiating the offense to either players 2 or 5, you should reverse the wing guard and post positions. Players 3 and 4 will assume the wing guard positions at the foul-line extended and the wing guards will post-up low. Using "crack down" screens by the post men, the wing guards come out for the ball and select the options available at that point. (Diagram 4-24)

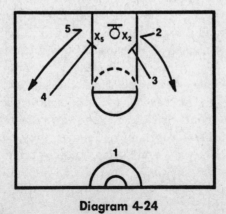

Diagram 4-24

Rebound Responsibilities

The rebound responsibilities in the Spread 1-2-2 are the same as in the other formations. The players, preferably our post men, are in low on each side of the lane, with either wing guard assuming the middle position, depending on which guard shoots. If player 1 shoots, the weakside wing guard should take middle-of-the-lane responsibility with the strongside wing guard getting back for defensive floor balance. These simple rules assure you of solid offensive rebounding with three-and-one-half men hitting the boards.

Spread 1-2-2 Delay-Game Offense

The Spread 1-2-2 Delay-Game Offense is a passing attack as well as a means of protecting a lead in a close ball game. If you can control the closing moments of your games, you will be victorious more often than not.

Advantages of the Spread Pattern

- The continuous pattern is easy to learn and execute.
- It is a team passing offense with little dribbling.
- It provides for the highest-percentage shots.
- The players without the ball are in constant motion.
- This movement takes the opposing team's big men away from the basket.
- The offense takes advantage of weak defenders.

When to Use the Delay Game Offense

Many coaches have divergent views on when to use delaying tactics. Many of these delaying tactics have "backfired" too many times, causing some coaches to have second thoughts about the delay-game offense. True, it is a gamble to change the tempo of the game this way, and lost momentum may never be regained with the regular offense.

However, there are times, usually late in the game and with a small lead, when the tempo should be changed, and a ball-control offense is in order. A rule of thumb is to go into the delay game when you are ahead by double the amount of time remaining. For example, if you are up by four points, with two minutes to go, that's when you should consider using the Delay-Game Offense.

Rules for the Delay-Game Offense

- Try to score with high-percentage shots.
- Use sharp V cuts when moving without the ball.
- Use crisp passes.
- Stay at least three feet from all out-of-bounds lines.
- All pass receivers must move toward the ball.
- Maintain 15-foot spacing.
- Maintain poise.
- Use your best ballhandlers.
- Avoid the double team.
- Apply pressure to the defense.

Alignment and Continuity

The alignment for the Delay-Game Offense is the Spread 1-2-2 with the players assuming their normal positions as dictated by the action of the regular Spread 1-2-2 Offense.

Player 1 is the point guard and sets up about six feet above the top of the key. Players 2 and 5 are the wing guards and station themselves about 12 feet from the foul line extended. Players 3 and 4 are the post men and set up about one step from the blocks. (Diagram 4-25)

The continuity starts with player 1 passing to the wing guard, player 2, who gets rid of his man and receives the pass. After passing to player 2, player

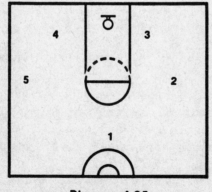

Diagram 4-25

1 uses a "crack down" screen on low post man 4's defender, allowing 4 to come up and to the left of the key. Meanwhile, when 2 received the initial pass, 3 moved out and away from the free-throw lane, allowing 5 to cut off 1's tail and post in the vacated spot left by player 3. (Diagram 4-26)

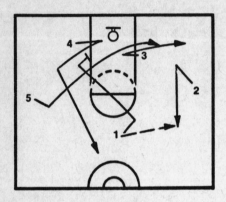

Diagram 4-26

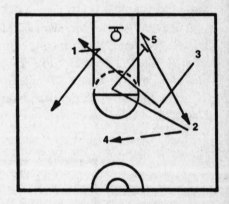

Diagram 4-27

Diagram 4-27 shows how the continuity is maintained with 2 swinging the ball to player 4 and screening down on 5's defender, player 3 cutting off 2's tail and player 1 moving out to the wing spot. Player 2 must be absolutely certain that he can complete his swing pass to 4 because an interception would be an easy two points for the opposition.

Continuity is maintained when 4 is unable to hit 3, who is cutting to the basket, by swinging the ball to 5 at the right of the key. Player 4 now screens down on 3's defender, with 1 cutting off 4's tail and replacing 2 who moves out to the wing position allowing 1 to post low. (Diagram 4-28)

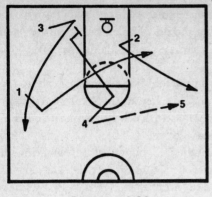

Diagram 4-28

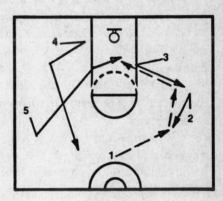

Diagram 4-29

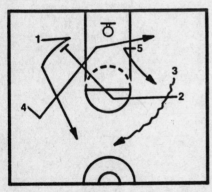

Diagram 4-30

We can increase the passing angle for the weakside cutters by having the strongside wing guard pass to the strongside post player and let the post player hit the cutter in close. (Diagram 4-29)

If 3 cannot hit the cutter, he dribbles out to the point as 2 moves across the lane and screens down for 1. Player 4 cuts off 2's tail and posts low, replacing 5, who moves out to the wing position as the motion continues. (Diagram 4-30)

Timing, skilled ballhandling and sharp cutting are necessary ingredients for the Delay-Game Offense. While you should insist on being patient, you should not hesitate to take the high-percentage shot if the defense gives it to you.

This offense can put your players on the foul line where they can ice the ball game. Practice is the key and you should allow at least ten minutes daily on your Delay-Game Offense. This offense, as with other passing and cutting offenses, will improve your man-for-man defense.

When practicing the Delay-Game Offense, you will also be working on your late-game defense in a suicide situation. Set up competitive games with points awarded to the offense for a certain number of completed passes and points awarded to the defense for any deflections or steals. Players like these competitive drills and it sharpens their defensive and offensive skills in a pressure situation.

The Delay-Game Offense is one of the most essential offenses to ensure the success of your team. It will provide you with another offense against superior teams.

With time running out in a close game, even the run-and-shoot coach would like to have sole possession of the ball. The Delay-Game Offense, with its motion and high-percentage scoring possibilities, has a definite role in basketball.

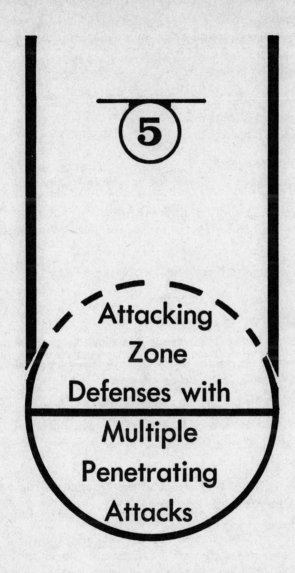

Attacking Zone Defenses with Multiple Penetrating Attacks

Zone Offense

When deciding what type of zone offense to use, you should evaluate your personnel first and determine how closely designed your man-for-man offense is to your zone attack.

Since more and more zone defenses are using man-for-man principles, it stands to reason that some man-for-man maneuvers will be effective against zone defenses. The closer the two attacks are in principle, the better the zone offense will be.

Next, you should consider why your opponent is using a zone defense. Most of the time, it's because the players lack mobility, but the following reasons should also be considered:

- To hide players who have difficulty playing man-for-man defense.
- To protect players in foul trouble.
- To change the game tempo.
- To protect a lead.
- To discourage good man-for-man offensive play.

Since these reasons are on the minus side, you can develop a positive attitude among your players and attack the zone defense with a positive point of view.

Suggested Factors for Team Play Versus Zone Defenses

- The players should be patient.
- Establish an inside game first.
- Look for the high-percentage shot with each possession.
- Use crisp passes; the overhead pass should be considered first and bounce passes can also be effective.
- Move to the ball and maintain 15-foot spacing.
- Use ball fakes before passing.
- Penetrate with ball and player movement.
- Get *behind* the defense.
- From 18 feet out, look to drive then pass inside. From inside 18 feet, look to shoot first.
- Rebound through the gaps in the zone.

There are some basic points in understanding zone defenses. The zone moves with the ball, permitting areas away from the ball to be open. Offensive players must position themselves in the seams of the zone, causing the defenders to split. At all times, the offensive players should think one pass ahead and know what to do with the ball before they get it. Also, defensive rebounders do not have specific block-out assignments, making it easier to rebound offensively.

Types of Zone Defenses

Basically, there are four types of zone defenses that a team will face: The standard sliding zones, the laning or stunting zones, the combinations and the zone presses.

The Standard Sliding Zones

The primary function of the standard sliding zones is to keep the ball away from the inside high-percentage scoring areas. They strive to pressure the ball out as much as possible without weakening their sagging wall near the basket. In effect, the sliding zones will permit perimeter passing. The standard zones are set in 2-1-2, 2-3, 1-2-2, 1-3-1 and 3-2 formations.

The Laning or Stunting Zones

The origin of the laning or stunting zones is the same as the sliding zones except that they are more aggressive in pressuring the ball and the passing lanes near the ball. Because these stunting zones apply more pressure on the ballhandler, it is necessary for the defense to be recognized and for adjustments to be adhered to. Otherwise, the offense may find itself having difficulty with its execution and be vulnerable to turn-overs.

Combination Zones

The combination zones usually mean the box-and-one, diamond-and-one, triangle-and-two and the matchup ones. The box and diamond are four-man zones with a chaser on the offense's best scorer. The triangle and two is a three man zone with two offensive players being played man-for-man. Over the past ten years, the matchup zone has proven difficult to counter.

The matchup may be of man-for-man origin or zone origin. The idea behind it is to have one-on-one coverage while presenting it as a zone defense. It is only man-for-man in that each defender is responsible for an offensive player when the offensive player enters that defender's area. He will not chase an offensive player all over the court, but will release him to another defender based on the defensive rules and still maintain the one-on-one coverage. While the matchup is more difficult to teach, it can be even more difficult to solve. However, the matchup zones have their own problems if the offense is designed to utilize a lot of player and ball movement.

Zone Presses

The zone presses used as a surprise element can turn a close game into a rout. They may extend full-court, three-quarter court or half-court. Whether the zone press originates from a 1-2-1-1, 2-2-1, matchup, or other alignment, the tempo is drastically changed, and even the most disciplined offenses can become unglued, with disastrous results.

Offensive Principles Versus
Zone Defenses

Regardless of what initial zone alignment is used, all zone defensive slides are the same after the basic ball and player movement has started. At least one defensive player is on the ball, one player is positioned near the post and at least one player defends the goal area against the weakside flow. As a result, in every zone defense, at least three of the defenders are fairly stationary. Because of this, the offensive players need to be able to read the defense and fill the seams of the zone, creating triangular passing angles through the overload principle.

Against the zone defenses, the offensive team should not allow the five defenders enough time to set up. The offense should attempt to fast break or look for the high-percentage shot upon every possession.

By design, the offense should attempt to spread the zone and pass behind it. This over-extension of the zone defense will structurally weaken its coverage and increase its vulnerability to the high-percentage shots. Through the use of ball fakes and dribble-punching, the zone can be frozen, allowing the ball to be reversed with high-percentage shot potential.

The offensive post area should be active, causing concern by the defense and allowing for baseline screening for the weakside cutters. Cutting through the zone with quick, well-coordinated movement is important, because added pressure is put on the defense since every cutter is a logical pass receiver and shooter. A good passer in the high post is an added asset, because he forces the defense to collapse (leaving the wings open). Also, the ball can be reversed quickly from the high post, keeping the defense a step behind, which allows for high-percentage shots.

All offensive players should time their cuts and penetrate into open areas away from the flow of the zone. An important point is to move the ball quicker than the zone can shift. It is this counter maneuver, against the flow of the zone, that will pick the defense apart.

Fundamental Concepts Versus
Zone Defenses

When you understand the different tactics of each zone and the zone strategies for meeting them, your players will then be able to successfully execute against the various zone defenses. Here are some fundamental concepts that should be emphasized when preparing the offense to meet zone defenses.

Passing

Since fewer offensive one-on-one skills are necessary when facing zone defenses, you should place great emphasis on your team's passing game. You've heard coaches say to move the ball when playing against the zones, but many times there isn't any purposeful passing that will lead to the good shot. The ball remains on the perimeter; when this happens, the zone isn't being tested. While it may be true that good outside shooting will make most teams come out of their zones, it's the clever passing and the player placement and movement that will lead to high-percentage shots.

Because the zone defenses zero-in on the ball, quick, accurate, pinpoint ball movement is a must in spreading the zone, which makes it more vulnerable. In your passing game with your fast break, you should insist that your players maintain 15-foot spacing. This concept forces your players to meet each pass, which maintains better floor balance.

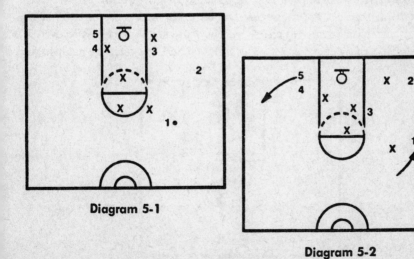

Diagram 5-1

Diagram 5-2

Overloading and Triangular Passing

Since zone defenses are ball defenses—that is, at least one man plays the ball, while the other four are defending areas without specific man coverage—you will be able to take the advantage by outnumbering (overloading) the defenders in certain areas with offensive personnel, thus setting up passing triangles. For example, in Diagram 5-1, the Basic Inside-Out formation has a built-in triangle with players 1, 2 and 3. If player 2 moves baseline and player 1 rotates to fill the vacated area, you still have the defense outnumbered 3 to 2. (Diagram 5-2)

Developing Passing Lanes

Consideration at this point must be given to developing the passing lanes. It is not enough merely to spread out on offense, since it can be spread too far. If the defense is not forced to move, its effectiveness can be doubled. Therefore, the offense must move the defense to create passing-lane openings. In order to create these openings, the offense must give serious consideration to the following points: 1) When the ball is high, the wing men must stay wide. This is especially important for the weakside players. 2) Rotate to a vacated spot and to the ball when a teammate cuts through the defense. This is mandatory for the ball-reversal maneuver. 3) Step into the seams of the zones, which splits the defenders and creates triangular passing possibilities.

Ball-Reversal Maneuver (Screening Baseline)

The Ball-Reversal Maneuver is the Baseline Series or weakside move. The success of any zone offense can be based on its ability to reverse the ball to the weakside, which takes advantage of a defensive player who has not recovered and is unable to defend his area. The Baseline Series is effective against all

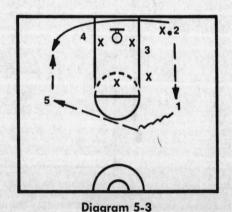

Diagram 5-3

zones because a screen is set along the baseline and places the offensive man in a one-on-one situation against his defender. You should be consistently strong along the baseline, and all of your attacks should incorporate this baseline maneuver.

Diagram 5-3 illustrates player 2 getting into the Baseline Series with 1 quickly reversing the ball to 5, who will look for 2 or 4 along the baseline. By doing so, you are taking a strength of the zone, the front, and negating it by attacking the side of the court.

Pressure the High and Low Posts

Establishing an inside game against the zone defense should be one of the first concerns for the offense. You should have at least one of your post men move high, then low; this keeps the defense honest and causes openings under the basket. Action at the high post is important for several reasons: the ball can be reversed easily from that area, the defense is usually without weakside help and a good passer at the high post can pass to the wings or directly to the low-post players. Every third or fourth pass should be in the high-post area.

Penetration Against the Zones

No team will consistently win from 18 to 25 feet out. The following maneuvers have been developed to penetrate the zone and move in for the high-percentage shots: dribble-punch and dribble-reverse, drive and cutting.

You have probably heard coaches saying to their players "Don't dribble against the zone, pass the ball". Purposeful passing is important, but so is the dribble. You shouldn't have players handle the ball excessively, but they should dribble-punch the ball at the defense, causing it to pinch and leave passing lanes open. In Diagram 5-4, player 1 dribbles (punches) the ball two or

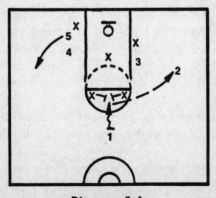

Diagram 5-4

three times at the defense in hopes of pinching the two top defenders, neither of whom is guarding him straight up. As 1 penetrates the gap, the two defenders converge on him, leaving the wings open for a pass and quick shot.

The dribble-reverse maneuver is illustrated in Diagram 5-5. Its purpose is to extend the defenders to the limit of their individual coverage areas, then reverse the ball to its original starting point. The wing guard, player 2, dribbles to his right, forcing X₁ to the limit of his area. Player 1 rotates to fill for 2 and receives a return pass from him. Player 5 rotates high to fill for 1, leaving X₂ with two offensive players to defend. Player 1 may have a quick shot or he can pass to 5, who may also be open.

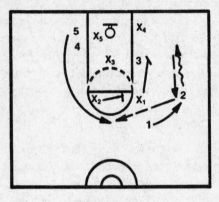

Diagram 5-5

Failure to penetrate allows the defense to defend the offensive players with little effort, making it difficult to initiate the offensive attack. While the direct pass is usually the easiest means of penetration, it may be the most difficult to execute against the better zones.

Upon receipt of any pass, instruct your players to assume the triple-threat position. Although you should try to pass after making fakes tell your players to look for any driving opportunities that may be available. Solid, driving, penetrating moves lead to good passes and high-percentage shots inside. These drives must be intelligent maneuvers with the players maintaining good body control and balance. Wild, impractical moves, lead to turn-overs or poor shots. Penetration against the zones can put the offensive players on the foul line. But, in order to get there, purposeful penetration is an important prerequisite.

When cutting against zones, the players must read the seams that are open and not just head for predetermined spots. Standing still after cutting leads to congestion. If a player doesn't receive the ball after cutting, he should look to set up another overload or return to his original spot.

Types of Cuts

The type and direction of the cuts can keep the defense guessing. Three types of cuts can be used in your offensive attacks. These cuts are illustrated in Diagrams 5-6 through 5-8. They are the post roll cut, the straight or right-angle cut and the X-cut.

With these cutting combinations, it is difficult for the defense to know where your cutters will be, where they're going, where they came from and how quick they are moving.

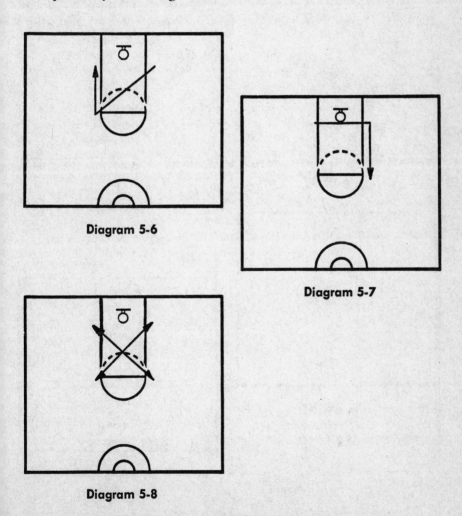

Diagram 5-6

Diagram 5-7

Diagram 5-8

Formations Against the
Various Zones

There are many types of zones and methods of attacking them. It would be impractical to develop and expect the players to execute a separate offense for each zone defense. Therefore, the zone defenses are separated into three categories: even-front zones, odd-front zones and combinations.

Any zone which shows two defenders at the top is designated as an even front (2-1-2, 2-3). Whenever a single defender is at the top of the key, it is designated an odd-front zone (1-3-1, 1-2-2, 3-2).

Against the even-front zones, attack with the Basic Inside-Out Offense, High 1-4 or Spread 1-2-2. The high 1-4 can also be adjusted to a Medium 1-4 formation.

When facing an odd-front zone, especially the 1-3-1, use the High 1-4. When being defensed with the 1-2-2 zone, use the Basic Inside-Out or a Medium 1-4.

This type of positioning permits the offensive players to split the defenders, making it easier to initiate the offensive movements. Furthermore, it creates uncertainty on the part of the individual defender in regard to where his defensive responsibility lies. Diagrams 5-9 through 5-12 illustrate this principle of splitting the defense.

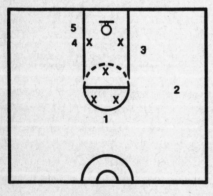

Diagram 5-9
Basic Inside-Out
vs 2-1-2

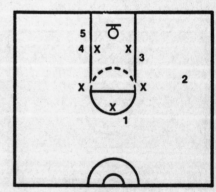

Diagram 5-10
Basic Inside-Out
vs 1-2-2

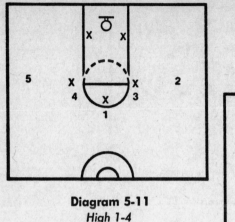

Diagram 5-11
High 1-4
vs 1-2-2

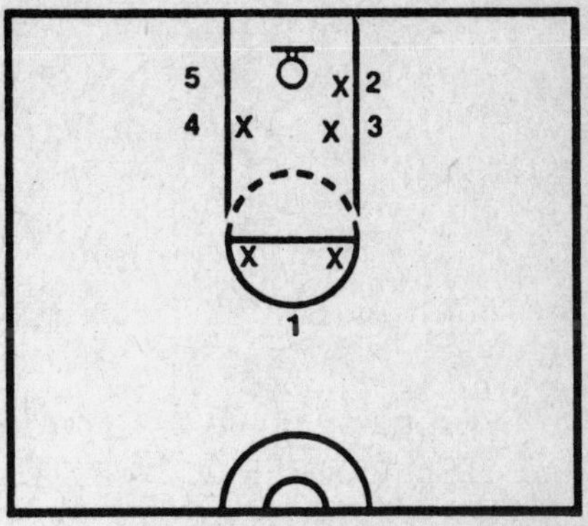

Diagram 5-12
Double Low Stack vs
Box-and-one combination

The Basic Inside-Out Offense Versus Even-Front Zones

The Basic Inside-Out Offense is an excellent offensive attack to use against most of the zone defenses you will encounter.

Some of the reasons for using the Basic Inside-Out Offense against the zone defenses are:

- It is difficult to match up against it without going straight man-for-man.
- It provides for excellent pass entries.
- It provides quick, high-percentage shots for all the players.
- It creates the overload principle through sound player and ball movement.
- It establishes an explosive inside game.
- It is a continuity attack with free-lance possibilities.
- It provides for excellent offensive rebounding.

Point to Wing Guard. The first entry used against even-front zones is for the point guard, player 1, to hit the wing guard, player 2, who is set up in the seam of the zone. If 2 is open, he can shoot or he can hit 3 in the side post and then move baseline. Player 1 rotates to fill 2's vacated spot. (Diagram 5-13)

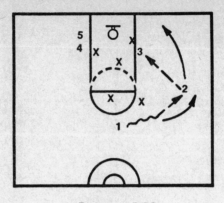

Diagram 5-13

Another very effective move is the pass from player 3 to player 2, who is moving baseline. Player 2 dribbles baseline then makes a hook pass to 3, who has stepped out. This move is effective because the baseline defender must honor 2's one-on-one move, leaving 3 open as he steps out. From this spot, player 3 can take the short jumper or make a strong penetrating move to the goal. (Diagram 5-14) Diagram 5-14 shows 3 returning the ball to 2 as he continues baseline. If the middle man is slow sliding down, player 2 then has an easy layup.

<u>Getting Into the Baseline Series.</u> If none of 2's aforementioned options are available, he returns the ball to 1 who reverses to 5 in the weakside wing. Player 5 can shoot or hit 2 as he is coming around a screen set by 4 on the bottom defender. (Diagram 5-15) If the defender breaks 4's screen, player 5 can hit 4 deep, or if 2 has the ball, he can "jam-it" in close to 4 for his baseline power move.

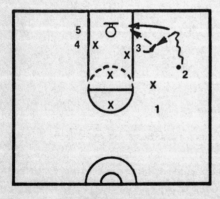

Diagram 5-14

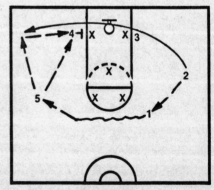

Diagram 5-15

Post Roll-and-Exchange. Diagram 5-16 illustrates the Post Roll-and-Exchange maneuver. Player 4, seeing that 2 cannot get the ball into him deep, uses a lateral cut and posts up on the opposite side of the lane as 3 flashes high. He then rolls hard down the lane. Player 3 could conceivably receive a pass in the high or low post from either player 2 or 5. Note the overload principle and triangular passing created by the player and ball movement in this maneuver. The two post players should use a lateral cut and a right-angle cut.

Reversing to the Wing. You can maintain continuity if the Post Roll-and-Exchange maneuver fails to develop. Player 2 returns the ball to 5, cuts behind the zone and receives a baseline screen from 4. Player 1 quickly dribbles right, looking for 2 or 4 in deep if the defense breaks the screen. Player 2 may, if necessary, look for an opening and a high cut to the ball. (Diagram 5-17)

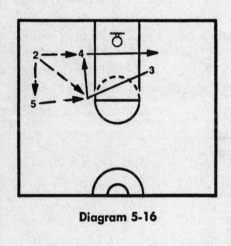

Diagram 5-16

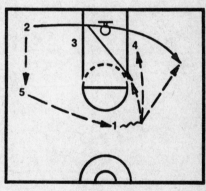

Diagram 5-17

Weakside Step-In. With the overload set on the wing reversal, player 5 can step in at the foul line, coming from the weakside, and have a nice 15-footer. All zones are vulnerable to weakside play, whether it's ball reversal or players cutting from the weakside. Player 5 can receive this pass from either player 2 or 1. Note the triangular passes available with the player and ball movement in this play. (Diagram 5-18)

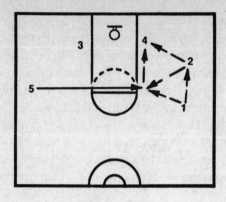

Diagram 5-18

<u>Weakside Series.</u> The Weakside Series is initiated on the side where players 4 and 5 are stacked. From this posture, the baseline defender can be split on the stack side with a 2-on-1 advantage. Player 5 pops out on an angle to receive the pass from player 1 as seen in Diagram 5-19. Player 5 may shoot, pass the ball into the post player, player 4, hit 2 coming over into the step-in spot or return the ball to the 1 man and get into the Baseline Series with player 3.

Diagram 5-19

If player 2 doesn't receive a pass from 5, he replaces himself, waiting for player 1's reversal of the ball. When 2 receives the pass from 1, he can shoot, dribble-punch the ball, pinch in the defenders and hit 5 coming around the screen set by player 3. If the bottom defender breaks 3's screen, player 2 can hit 3 in close for the high-percentage shot. (Diagram 5-20)

If none of these options are available, players 3 and 4 execute a post roll-and-exchange and continuity is maintained.

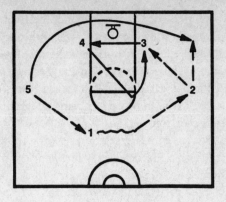

Diagram 5-20

"Jam-It" to the Big Man. The only real maneuver that is changed in the execution of the Inside-Out Zone Attack is the elimination of the pick-and-roll. Instead, player 3 posts himself along the side post and works with player 2 from that spot. Diagram 5-21 illustrates 2 "jamming-it" to 3 at the side post. From there, players 2 and 3 can work their two-man game with a give-and-go, hook-pass and power-shot inside.

Guard Cut. If you have a good-shooting guard, use the guard-cut option. Diagram 5-22 illustrates player 1 hitting the weakside wing guard, player 5, who has moved out to the wing position. Player 1 then cuts down and out to his left, using a screen set by player 4.

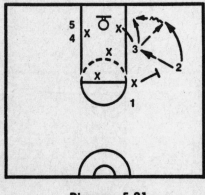

Diagram 5-21

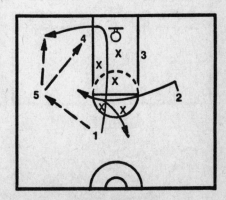

Diagram 5-22

There are two very important points which need emphasis here. First, timing is very important in allowing player 1 to get through and out to receive the pass from 5. Player 5 should dribble-pull the ball by moving toward the key, then reverse and look for player 1 or 4 inside. Second, player 2 must rotate to the top of the key for defensive balance in case of a turnover or fast break. He should, however, move to the step-in spot, being a logical pass receiver before assuming his defensive responsibility.

Spotting Up. Spotting up refers to the placement of the offensive players in the seams of standard zone defenses, then quickly moving the ball in triangles before the defense can slide and adjust to the ball.

In Diagram 5-23, the shaded areas represent the open areas in a 2-1-2 zone, and Diagram 5-24 illustrates how to rotate into the Spot-Up variation. The simple move of sending player 5 to the strongside corner functions on the overload principle and provides excellent triangular passing.

When player 1 brings the ball over half-court, he signals the spot-up, and the players assume their positions depending on what zone you are facing. The spot-up variation versus a 2-1-2 zone is illustrated in Diagram 5-25. Player 1 can start the spot-up maneuver by hitting 2, who can pass to 3 or 5 or back to 1 until a shot is obtained. The wing guards, players 2 and 5 should look inside first before they shoot or pass back.

To reverse the ball, player 4 moves out to the wing, player 5 slides across to the weakside corner, player 3 slides across the lane, player 1 moves into the step-in spot and player 2 stays low in offensive rebounding position. (Diagram 5-26)

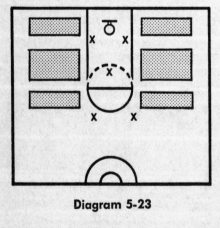

Diagram 5-23

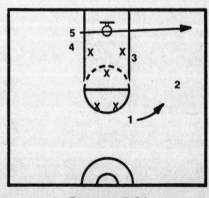

Diagram 5-24

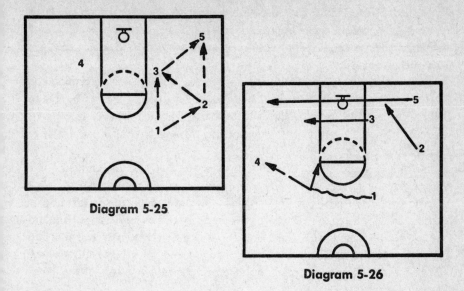

Diagram 5-25

Diagram 5-26

Meeting the Combination Zones

The Matchup Zones

The matchup zones were devised by defensive-minded coaches to negate the overloading and continuity-patterned offenses used against the sliding zones. The matchups attempt to use as many man-for-man principles as possible while maintaining a zone posture.

Since the matchup zones rely on rules governing defensive coverage, it would be impractical to design different offenses that would have to face various matchups with various sets of rules. As a result, you should rely on the system of Multiple Penetrating Attacks, which includes a 1-3-1 Passing-Game Offense against a matchup defense. As long as the offense has a lot of screening and cutting along with ball movement, the effectiveness of the matchup zone will be reduced. Offenses that rely only on ball movements will have difficulty solving the matchup.

The 1-3-1 Passing Game Offense Versus Matchup Defenses

The 1-3-1 Passing Game Offense can make significant contributions to your multiple alignment offensive system. While it is a departure from the patterned phase offenses, in that it is a free-lance offense, it is very effective against matchup and pressure man-for-man defenses. Its recent revival and popularity has caused many coaches to take a closer look at its concepts and ingredients.

The Passing Game is a team-oriented offense that emphasizes good player and ball movement, screening and an explosive inside game. It is a *ruled* free-lance offense that is not subjected to the stereotyping found in rigid patterned offenses.

Automatic keys based on ball and player positioning determine the offensive movements that develop later. Each offensive player must be able to "read" the defense, set up his man and cut with a purpose. Intelligent movement, based on rules and defensive mistakes is critical in the Passing-Game Attack.

Advantages of the 1-3-1 Passing Game. The 1-3-1 alignment has a very important advantage over an open key formation. By always having a player in the high-post position, weakside defensive help in the low post is eliminated. With a man in the high post, backdoor situations are available and the ball can be passed in all directions. By having players in both the high and the low post, you can constantly interchange these players, which is a very effective move against the matchup defense. Other advantages of the 1-3-1 Passing Game are:

- It is not a patterned offense, making it extremely difficult to scout.
- It is easily adjusted to your personnel, and it can be changed from game to game and from season to season.
- The Passing Game shows your players every situation they will see on defense. While you are working on the Passing Game, you will also be improving your defense.
- It is easy to get into the Passing Game from a fast-break situation. There is no need to set up the offense since any one of the players can assume any offensive position.
- It is difficult to apply defensive pressure to the Passing-Game Offense.

Passing Rules. There are basically five rules that your players should adhere to when passing the ball:

- Think pass.
- Always make the easy pass.
- Always pass *away from the* defenders.
- The ball should go to the high post on every third pass.
- The ball should be passed at least three or four times before a shot is taken, unless it is a layup.

Dribble Rules. There are four rules for dribbling situations that your players should adhere to:

- They can dribble to get a better passing angle to any other player.
- If they can get to the basket in two or three dribbles, they can go one-on-one.
- When a dribbler moves toward another offensive player, that player should clear out.
- Dribbling is permitted to maintain floor balance.

<u>General Rules</u>. You should develop your own general passing-game rules based on your personnel and on what your offensive intent is. The Passing Game is designed to obtain high-percentage shots with motion against any defense using man-for-man principles. Since the matchup zone uses man-for-man principles, the Passing Game's screening techniques, coupled with its ball and player movement, keeps the defense constantly moving. Here are the general rules for the Passing Game:

- Each offensive player must move every time a pass is made.
- Upon receipt of the ball, your players must assume the triple-threat position and look to pass, shoot or penetrate to the basket.
- Upon assuming the triple-threat position, your offensive player should hold the ball for at least a two-second count. This will allow time for things to develop inside.
- Do not move too fast. The players must set up their men, wait for screens and then move with a purpose. They must use the screens to get their shots.
- Unless the ball is at the low post, at least three or four passes should be made before a shot is taken. The defense *must* be moved.
- Each offensive player is limited to three dribbles unless he is trying to escape from trouble or to get a better passing angle.
- Every third pass should go to the high post.
- Always make the easy pass.
- Do not fight pressure. When overplayed, execute a backdoor cut or screen down for a player on the baseline.
- The player in the point position must defend against the fast break.

The general rules have been listed, each player must know what his responsibilities will be when he is in either post position or in a perimeter position.

<u>Post-Player Rules</u>. The following are rules for the post players:

- The high- and low-post players screen for each other if the high-post player doesn't receive the ball within a three-second count.

- The high-post player is on the ballside. The low-post player is on the side away from the ball, looking to screen for cutters.
- The high-post man should be one pass away (15 feet) from the ball.
- Post players should take the ball to the basket if the defense dictates such a move.
- When the ball is in the high post, that player should look inside, then look opposite (weakside) from where the pass came.
- When the high-post player passes to a perimeter player, he should: screen for the low post, screen for the opposite wing, slide low.
- When the ball is passed into the low post, that player should: look to score first, look for the high post rolling, look for a perimeter player.
- The high post must always be filled.
- All post players work for offensive rebound position.

<u>Perimeter-Player Rules.</u> The perimeter players are at the wing and point positions. There are three sets of rules that govern their movements: for players without the ball, players with the ball and for a player after passing the ball.

Players Without the Ball:

- Set up for screens using a change-of-direction move.
- Move to the ball.
- Screen away from the ball.
- When overplayed, execute a backdoor cut or screen down for a player along the baseline.
- Maintain 15-feet spacing.
- Use rear screens.
- Fill high post if vacated.
- Replace themselves.
- No two players can cut in the same direction simultaneously.
- When passing to the high post, the man must split the post with another player, either to his left or right.

Player With the Ball:

- Looks for the low post, then the high post man.
- Doesn't shoot until a post man has handled the ball, unless it is in the layup position.

- When in the baseline position, he avoids picking up his dribble.
- Dribbles to increase a passing angle or on a penetration move.
- Holds the ball for at least a two-second count.

Player After Passing the Ball:

- Cuts to the basket after using a change-of-direction move.
- Screens away from the ball after using a change-of-direction move.
- Screens on a player below when pressured, after using a change-of-direction move.
- Cuts to the baseline and away from the basket after using a change-of-direction move.

Teaching the Passing Game With Drills

When teaching any type of passing game, whether it's a three, four or five man passing offense, it is very important to actually overcoach the fundamentals of the offense. This is especially true when getting the players to move without the ball. Most of the action in the Passing Game occurs without the ball, therefore, it is necessary to constantly remind the players that purposeful movement away from the ball is a must if the Passing-Game Offense is to be successful.

You should reinforce the passing-game rules by breaking them down into simple drills that present the offense in parts, leading to the "whole concept." You should stress different points each day so that the players become familiar with game situations through recognition. Coach your players to act instinctively to the situations they face.

In most of the drills, player movement is preceded by a change-of-direction move. This makes the players think more about moving without the ball, and it makes them move with purposeful intent.

Because the Passing Game is a free-lance offense without predetermined movements, it would be very difficult to diagram. Therefore, only the drills that incorporate the basic offensive movements will be illustrated.

Pass-Screen Opposite Drill. Diagram 5-27 illustrates the Pass-Screen Opposite Drill. The players are divided into groups of threes, and for the first week to ten days, we won't use any defense. Player 1 passes to 2 and sets a back screen for 5, who should use the screen and look to shoot. After setting the screen, player 1 steps out into the wing position.

Step-In or Replace Drill. Diagrams 5-28 and 5-29 illustrate the Step-in or Replace Drill. Player 1 passes to 2 and screens opposite for 5, who moves to the top of the key and receives a return pass from 2. Player 5 then swings the ball to 1 who, in turn, looks for player 2 at the foul line. If player 2 doesn't receive the pass from 1, he must replace himself to maintain floor balance.

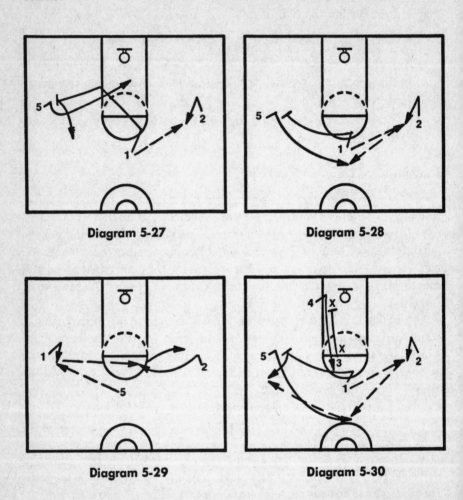

Diagram 5-27   Diagram 5-28

Diagram 5-29   Diagram 5-30

Post-Screen-Post Drill. The Post-Screen-Post Drill is illustrated in Diagram 5-30. In this drill, you should have defensive men on post players 3 and 4. The post players should move with a purpose, and having defenders on them makes them work harder to get the ball. Player 1 passes to 2 and screens opposite for 5. Player 5 moves out on top and gets a return pass from 2. Meanwhile, the post players are screening for each other until one of them gets open. The perimeter players keep passing and moving until one of them can get the ball to a post player, either high or low.

Rear-Screen Continuity Drill. The Rear-Screen Continuity Drill is shown in Diagrams 5-31 and 5-32. This is an excellent drill that incorporates the basics of the Passing Game: passing, screening and movement. The drill starts with 1 passing to 2 and screening opposite for player 5. Player 4 moves up and sets a rear screen for player 1, allowing him to cut to the basket as he anticipates a pass from 2. If 1 doesn't receive this pass, he posts up low on the opposite side. Player 2 reverses the ball to 5 who, in turn, swings it to 4 who has stepped out into the wing. Player 1 now sets a rear screen for 5 who anticipates the pass from player 4. If 5 doesn't receive this pass, he posts up low on the opposite side and the drill continues

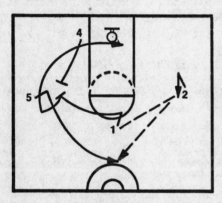

Diagram 5-31

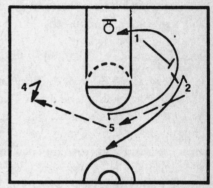

Diagram 5-32

In addition to the passing-game drills, we use several scrimmage situations to further aquaint our players with the principles of the Passing Game. Several of the rules are selected daily and emphasis is given to each through these mini-scrimmages.

The following are some of the scrimmage games that we play to help our players get acclimated to the rules of the Passing Game:

- Keep away: In this drill, the offense must complete seven consecutive passes to gain a point. The defense receives a point if it can deflect or intercept a pass within the first five. The game is to ten points, with the losers running sprints. This should be at least a 4-on-4 game.

- Ten passes and a layup: In this scrimmage drill, which is 5-on-5, the offense must make at least ten passes before a shot can be taken, and this shot must be a layup. Any violation of the rules turns the ball over to the defense, who then go on offense. The scrimmage is played till five baskets are made.

- Ten passes and certain player shoots: This drill is similar to the one above except that we call out the name of a player on each position and that player must shoot after ten passes or more. This shot must be his type of shot or a shot which is considered a good percentage shot for that player.

- 4-on-4 scrimmage: In this scrimmage game, no dribbling or shooting from outside is allowed. Instead we emphasize certain rules and stress passing, screening and moving without the ball. We don't use a post player but insist that the post be filled. This scrimmage can be timed or to a certain number of baskets.

The best way to negate the match-up defense is with movement. Defensive coverage becomes increasingly more difficult with the passing, cutting and screening techniques that the Passing Game Offense stresses.

The Box-and-One, Diamond-and-One and the Triangle-and-Two

Diagrams 5-33 to 5-35 illustrate the possible postures for the Box-and-one, Diamond-and-one and the Triangle-and-two. These combination defenses are used occasionally , but you had better be prepared to meet them at any time, especially if you have one or two star players. In the Box-and-one, the wings and high post are open for player placement and movement.

Diagram 5-33 shows the posture of the Box-and-one, with the shaded area forming a "box zone" with the circled X defender playing man-for-man on 2 in the Basic Inside-Out alignment. The Box-and-one is usually used against a two-guard offense so it can match up out front easier.

Diagram 5-34 illustrates a Diamond-and-one posture. The diamond formation matches up better when the offense has a one-guard front. In the diamond, the corners and high post are open for player placement and movement.

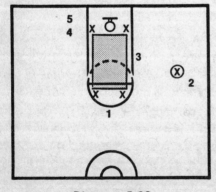

Diagram 5-33

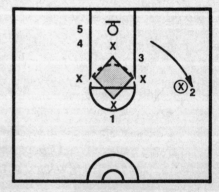

Diagram 5-34

In Diagram 5-35, the Triangle-and-two is illustrated using a three man zone coupled with two chasers. In the Diagram, players X1 and X2 are playing man-for-man on 1 and 2, while X3, X4 and X5 are forming a triangular zone. These combination defenses, unless given a lot of practice time, can backfire even when they are used as surprise elements against the offense. Because they are combinations, and not totally basic to one defense, they are extremely vulnerable to mixups in coverage. If faced with any of these combinations, you should attack them with a positive attitude, because their structure and coverage is not airtight.

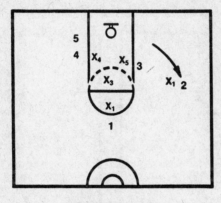

Diagram 5-35

Attacking the Combinations

For simplicity, I will illustrate the Box-and-one combination, and the method of attacking it. You should attack the Diamond the same way. Sometimes, we will run the Passing Game against the Triangle-and-two. It's a matter of pitting your strengths against the weaknesses of the defense.

The Stack Versus the Box-and-One. You should use the Double Low Stack when faced with a combination defense that is trying to stop your best scorer (usually player 2). There are several reasons for this: First, it's one of the Multiple Penetrating attacks and a new pattern doesn't have to be learned to meet this defense. Second, you won't have any difficulty getting the ball to your best shooter. Third, all the players have the same scoring opportunities. Fourth, it's not a physically exhausting offense for the high scorer. Finally, the stack provides penetration from the point, and a power-game inside.

The basic idea in this offense is to free your best shooter, while still incorporating the other four players into the offense as scoring threats. It should be easy to split the box in the middle by flashing players into that area. Many shots will occur from the wing spots as well.

Diagram 5-36 shows the Double Low-Stack alignment, with player 2 being played man-for-man. Player 2, the wing guard, is stacked with a big man, player 3, on the right side, and 5, the other wing guard, is stacked with the other big man, player 4, on the left. Player 1 can start the offense to either side.

If the point guard dribbles right, player 3 screens the defender on player 2, allowing 2 to lose his man. (Diagram 5-37) Player 2 can shoot, "jam-it" in low to 3, execute a pick-and-roll with 3 or return the ball to 1 and get into the Baseline Series. By stacking the big men low, you are in excellent position to control the offensive board. The bottom men playing the zone will take themselves out of rebounding position because of their defensive slides.

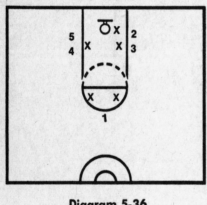

Diagram 5-36

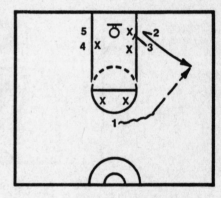

Diagram 5-37

If 2 returns the ball to player 1, player 5 flashes into the middle of the box and looks for the jump-shot near the foul-line. He can also penetrate and dish off to either 3 or 4 if one or both of the low men pick him up. (Diagram 5-38)

If 5 can't shoot or penetrate, he passes back to 1, who has rotated to his left for balance, and 1 looks for 2 who is rubbing his defender off a screen set by 4. (Diagram 5-39)

Player 2 can shoot or "jam-it" to 4 for a one-on-one baseline move. If 2 cannot shoot or hit 4 low, player 4 clears out and executes a Post Roll-and-Exchange with 3. Meanwhile, 5 has stacked with 3 on the right side. (Diagram 5-40)

If 2 returns the ball to 1 without executing his options, he cuts low toward the right side of the court, rubbing his man off 4. Meanwhile, player 5 pops out, looking for a pass from 1. Player 4 can move into the lane, also looking for a penetrating pass from 1. Player 5 has the same options as 2, and continuity is maintained. (Diagram 5-41)

When confronted with a combination defense from this type of posture, your best shooter will face few problems in obtaining his shots. In addition, your other players get high-percentage shots in close as a result of the open seams left in the box.

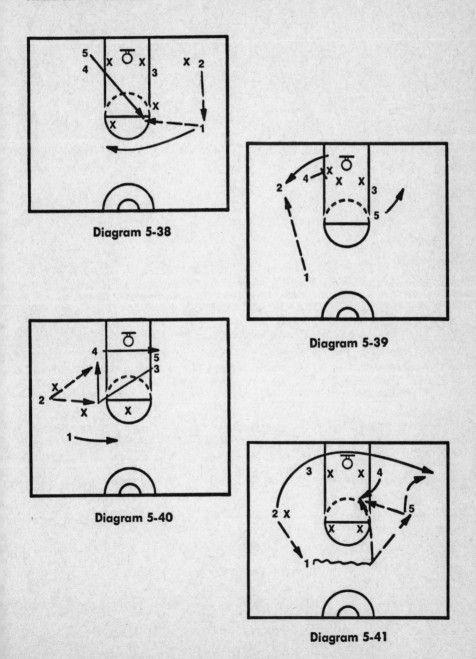

Diagram 5-38

Diagram 5-39

Diagram 5-40

Diagram 5-41

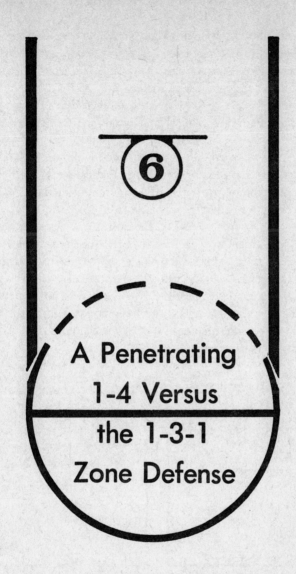

6

A Penetrating 1-4 Versus the 1-3-1 Zone Defense

Popularity of the 1-3-1 Zone Defense

The popularity and success that the 1-3-1 zone defense has enjoyed in recent years against conventional zone offenses warrants its receiving special attention in this chapter.

The huge success that the university and college ranks have had in using the 1-3-1 zone has influenced more high school coaches to explore its versatility.

Universities like North Carolina and Kentucky have used the 1-3-1 zone with different postures and strategies; containing, laning, stunting, trapping and matchup principles have not only made the 1-3-1 zone versatile but have made it very difficult to solve. Teams that employ the 1-3-1 usually have three mobile, big men spread across the free-throw line extended and at least one quick, aggressive guard pressuring the ball, making it difficult to initiate the offensive attack.

From this posture, the 1-3-1 defense maintains a strong wall inside and is an excellent rebounding defense for a zone. Because of its strengths in the middle and strong rebounding potential, teams that like to fast break find that the 1-3-1 is conducive to fast break basketball. (Diagram 6-1)

When playing against the 1-3-1, the offensive wings are covered by the defensive wingmen, making it difficult to obtain medium-range shots, and it is sometimes difficult to get behind the defense in order to get the important baseline shots where the 1-3-1 is weakest. The offensive team may also find itself stymied when it tries to beat the 1-3-1 zone with ball-reversal tactics. With the baseline runner, wingmen and top guard defending the ball in the corner, it is extremely difficult to pass the ball back out as the 1-3-1 jams the normal passing lines. (Diagram 6-2)

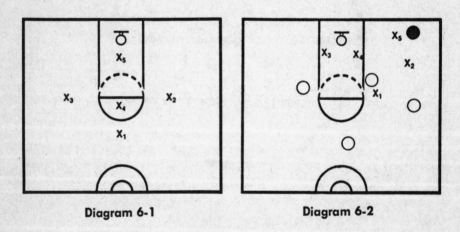

Diagram 6-1   Diagram 6-2

Meeting and Countering the 1-3-1
Zone Defense

After some experimentation, the 1-4 alignment has been found to be the best counter to the 1-3-1. The 1-4, illustrated in Diagram 6-3, shows that the defenders are outnumbered four to three across the foul line, providing the point guard with four entries to start the offensive attack. This numerical advantage forces each defender to make a decision as to which offensive player he must defend.

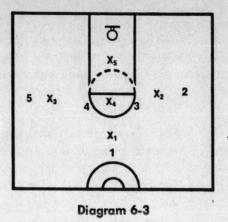

Diagram 6-3

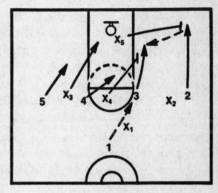

Diagram 6-4   **Diagram 6-5**

Advantages of the 1-4 Against the 1-3-1

Regardless of which offensive player the defenders choose to overplay, one offensive man will always be free. The 1-4 will always provide a two-on-one advantage for the offensive team against the 1-3-1 zone defense.

Another advantage that the 1-4 has against the 1-3-1 is that the baseline runner is wasted as a defender against any of the four entry passes. As a result, he will sometimes cheat up to put the defense in a man-for-man situation. This, too, would be to your advantage, because the defenders would be defending with little weakside help.

The 1-4 alignment provides for easy reversal of the ball, a necessary offensive tactic against any zone defense. The ball can be passed point-to-wing, back to the point or wing-to-point-to-wing. If the top defender overplays the point guard, the weakside wing can move over to help, or he can hit the strongside post, who can then reverse the ball. (Diagram 6-4)

In addition, the 1-4 isolates the baseline defender by forcing him to play a man in the corner, opening the low post. For example, in Diagram 6-5, player

1 passes to the high post, player 3, who hits 2 in the corner. This will force the baseline defender out, allowing 3 to roll in low for a quick return pass before X₄ can move down to front 3 from the baseline side. This maneuver places player 3 in an advantageous position for a strong power-move to the basket.

Initiating the 1-4 Attack–Guard Entries

With the placement of four offensive players extending out from the foul line, the point guard has four entry passes from which to choose in order to initiate the offensive attack. As in the other multiple alignments, the player positioning remains the same. The right side is the strongside and the left side is the weakside. (Diagram 6-6)

As the wing guards, players 2 and 5, position themselves near the foul-line extended, the posts, players 3 and 4, straddle the circle at the key. You should insist that the post players position themselves at least one full step above the foul line to avoid the lane violation.

The four basic entries for the point guard are: pass to the strongside wing (player 2), pass to the weakside wing (player 5), pass to the strongside post (player 3) and pass to the weakside post (player 4).

Pass to the Strongside Wing. Each entry pass *keys* the option which is to take place. In Diagram 6-7, player 1 passes to the wing guard, player 2, who returns the ball to the point and cuts behind the zone to the weakside corner. The return pass to the point keys the weakside post, player 4, to slide down the free-throw lane and screen the baseline defender, enabling the wing guard, player 2, to receive a pass from 5 as 1 reverses the ball to him.

Player 1 now sets up in player 4's position at the foul line, and the strongside post, player 3, moves down the lane on his side for offensive rebound position. In Diagram 6-8, the positioning of players 2,4,5, and 1 provides a nice overload situation, adhering to the zone principles of ball-reversal and player and ball movement.

The shooting options from this maneuver are as follows: corner shot by 2, power move inside by 4, medium-range jumper by 5 at the wing position, jumper by 1 at the foul line or a close-in shot by 3 on a pass from 1.

Pass to the Weakside Wing. The pass to the weakside wing is the reversal of the first option mentioned. In Diagram 6-9, player 1 passes to the wing guard, player 5, who looks to the post player, player 4, first, then passes back to the point guard. The point guard then swings the ball to player 2. The post player, player 3, slides down and screens off the baseline defender as 5 cuts to the corner, anticipating 2's pass. The weakside post, player 4, slides down for offensive rebounding position as 1 cheats in at the foul line. The shooting options from this maneuver are as follows: corner-shot by 5, power-move by 3 in close, medium-range jumper by 2 at the wing or a jumper from the foul line by 1, cheating in.

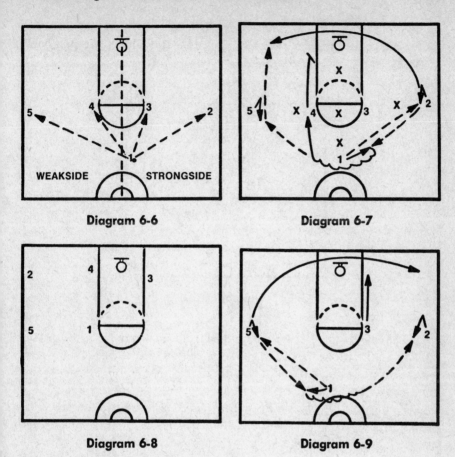

Diagram 6-6

Diagram 6-7

Diagram 6-8

Diagram 6-9

Pass to the Strongside Post. The pass to the strongside post is shown in Diagram 6-10. This maneuver offers many offensive scoring opportunities. Player 1 gives the strongside post, player 3, a semi-lob pass. You should instruct your guards to use the semi-lob for two reasons. First, the middle and strongside wing defenders won't have any opportunity for interception or deflection of a lower pass. Second, the semi-lob is a much easier pass to handle than a low hard pass. You want your post men to go up and get the ball, rather than wait for it to come to them. This is a basic principle for all pass receivers, that is, to come and meet each pass.

Upon receipt of this pass, player 3 has two options: he can shoot or he can pass to 2 who will head for the right corner. If he passes to 2, 3 slides low for a power shot. (Diagram 6-10) Note that 1 rotates to fill for 2, and 5 rotates to fill in for 1 at the point. Player 4, meanwhile, slides low in anticipation of the offensive rebound.

As the defensive players pinch on 3 at the key, player 4, sliding low, may be open for a close-in shot, and 5 is often open at the weakside wing as X3 slides down to help in the lane. The high-post players are instructed to face the basket immediately upon receipt of any pass. This applies pressure on the defense.

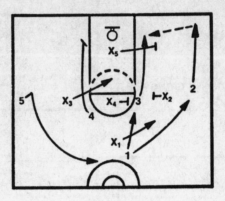

Diagram 6-10

The ball can also be reversed, as shown in Diagram 6-11, with 2 passing back to 1 who swings the ball to 5. Player 5 passes to 2, who is coming off the baseline screen set by 4. Player 5 then cheats in at the foul line as 4 sets himself for a power-move inside.

Pass to the Weakside Post. Diagram 6-12 illustrates the pass to the weakside post. The point guard gives the post, player 4, a semi-lob pass with the wing guard, player 5, sliding to the left corner as 4 pivots and faces the basket. Player 4 has the option to shoot or to pass to 5, who heads for the corner, after which 4 slides low. If 5 cannot shoot, he must look for 4, who is sliding low and looking for a power-shot in close. If 4 cannot hit 5, he should look immediately to the strongside wing, player 2, who may be slipping behind X2 for a medium-range jumper. As the high-post defender pinches on 4, player 3 can slip behind him and have a nice ten-foot shot in the lane.

Let's assume that 5 has the ball in the corner on 4's first option. Diagram 6-13 shows 4 sliding low, looking for 5's pass in close. With the ball in the corner, player 1 rotates to fill in for 5 and 2 rotates to fill in for 1 at the top of the key.

If 5 cannot shoot or hit 4 in deep, he passes back to 1 and cuts along the baseline. Player 1 reverses the ball to the wing guard, player 2, who looks for 5 coming off a baseline screen set by 3. Player 3 had moved down for offensive rebound position from the high post when 5 had the ball in the corner. (Diagram 6-14) Player 2 now jumps in the wing spot, following his pass, and 1 cheats in at the foul line.

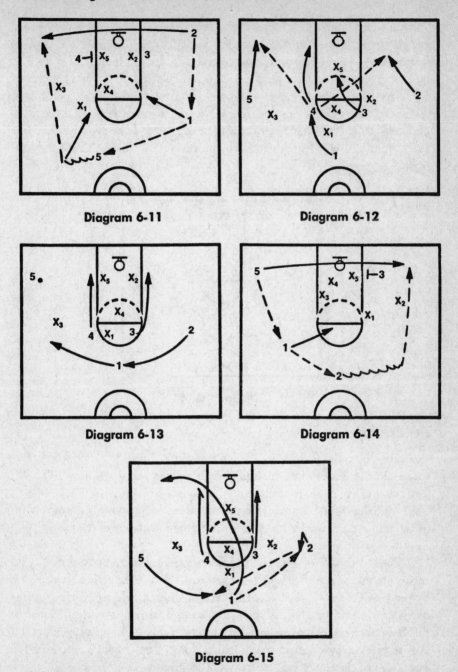

Diagram 6-11

Diagram 6-12

Diagram 6-13

Diagram 6-14

Diagram 6-15

Guard Cut. If player 1 is a good shooter, you should use the guard cut. It provides him with a nice baseline shot. Diagram 6-15 shows the guard-cut maneuver with 1 passing to wing guard 2 and cutting for the left corner.

Player 5 rotates high as 2 reverses the ball to him. Player 4 slides down low and screens the baseline defender as well as positioning himself for the close-in power-move. Player 5, after taking several dribbles to his left, looks for 1 in the corner. Player 4 may be open if X₅ breaks his screen, so 5 must be alert and not hurry his pass to 1. Player 4, if open, would have the higher percentage shot. Remember, from this position, if the low man wants the ball, he must "explode" to it. This maneuver can also be mirrored to the opposite side, but you should let the defense dictate which side is more vulnerable for penetration. (Diagram 6-16)

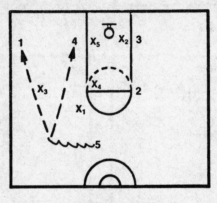

Diagram 6-16

The 100 Series

The 100 series is a continuity pattern against the 1-3-1 and incorporates the baseline series, the post roll-and-exchange and reversal of the ball. The 100 series can be signalled from the bench, or by player 1, and it can be executed from both sides of the key until the defense adjusts. The movements of the 100 Series are keyed either by a pass to a wing guard or to one of the post players from the point guard.

Pass to the Wing Guard. In Diagram 6-17, player 1 passes to 2, who shoots or makes a return pass to 1 and gets into the baseline series. He does this by heading for the opposite corner. Player 4 slides low to screen the baseline defender as 1 swings the ball to 5. The wing guard, player 5, can shoot or dribble-punch the ball in order to hit 2 in the corner or 4 in the low post. If 2 does receive the pass, he can shoot, look inside to 4 or look for 3 executing the post roll-and-exchange as 4 clears out. (Diagram 6-18)

If 2 cannot connect on any of these options, he passes back to 5, who reverses the ball to 1. Meanwhile, player 2 cuts along the baseline and uses a screen set by 4 to get open in the opposite corner. Player 1 takes several dribbles and looks for 2 in the corner or 4 in the low post. Players 1 and 5 both move in for shooting possibilities at the foul line. (Diagram 6-19)

Pass to the Pivot. The same continuity can be executed from a pass to a post man. In Diagram 6-20, player 1 hits the post, player 3, who pivots and looks for 2 cutting to the goal. If 2 is not open, player 3 passes to either 1 or 5, who then looks for 2 as he gets into the baseline series with 4.

If the ball goes to 2 in the corner and 2 cannot shoot or hit 4 in deep, players 4 and 3 execute the post roll-and exchange, previously illustrated in Diagram 6-18. If this option is unavailable, player 2 returns the ball to 5. (Diagram 6-19) These options can be mirrored to the opposite side of the floor.

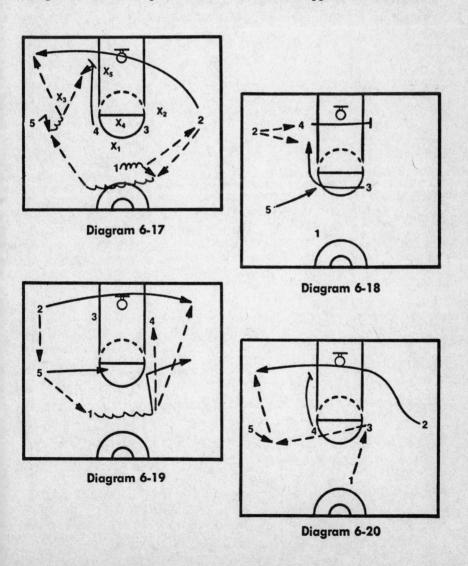

Diagram 6-17

Diagram 6-18

Diagram 6-19

Diagram 6-20

Rebound Responsibilities

Basically, the offensive rebounding responsibilities for the players executing the 1-4 attack against the 1-3-1 zone defense are the same as they are in the other multiple attacks. The off-side post will always be in offensive rebound position away from the ball, with the other post assuming his duties on the ball side.

The off-side wing will have middle-rebound duties, while the player at the point anticipates long rebounds as well as protecting against a fast break.

The 1-4 is very effective against the 1-3-1 zone. It provides high-percentage shots for your best shooters, a power-game inside, the overload principle and excellent offensive rebounding position.

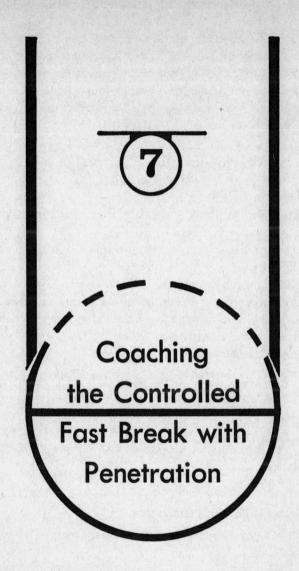

7

Coaching the Controlled Fast Break with Penetration

The fast break is your first offensive option and probably the most potent weapon in basketball. With basketball players being bigger, stronger, quicker and faster than at any other time, it is no wonder that the fast break is in the offensive repertoire of nearly every coach on the high school and collegiate levels.

The Controlled Fast Break provides the offense with a quick-hitting transition offense which can erupt quick turnover baskets and total control of the game.

There are two important points that usually turn a game around. One is gap time and the other is spurt time. Gap time refers to holding your opponents scoreless on a certain number of possessions. Spurt time refers to your scoring five or six straight baskets while your opponents are in gap time. The fast break can spearhead this spurt from either your defense or your Controlled Fast Break Offense.

Psychological Effect on the Opposition

The Controlled Fast Break puts great pressure on the opposition, causing them to think about getting back on defense while they are still on offense.

Also, the fast break forces opposing teams to play a more deliberate game, which can have a negative effect on their players. In addition, the opponent's offensive rebounding will slacken as the players become preoccupied with getting back on defense before the fast break can be executed.

The fast break leads to more aggressive team defense; a defense that is extremely alert, coming up with many loose balls through aggressive rebounding, which is instrumental in causing turnovers.

Advantages of the Controlled Fast Break

The Controlled Fast Break possesses the following advantages over a run-and-gun type of break:

- It reduces errors in execution and cuts down on turnovers.
- It produces high-percentage shots.
- It allows you to substitute freely, giving most of your players an opportunity to play.
- It weakens your opponent's offensive rebounding, allowing you to get the break started.
- It's a great crowd pleaser and today's players like to run it.
- It makes your defense more aggressive as your players realize they can score easy fast-break baskets off their defense.
- It provides scoring opportunities for all the players because it is a controlled break with specific player responsibilities.
- It is a great motivational factor.
- It keeps the players in peak condition and develops stamina.
- Your best ball handler will control the break most of the time.

Organizing the Controlled Fast Break

In organizing the Controlled Fast Break, the first thing to do is to divide the court lengthwise into five areas. These five areas are designated as lanes and alleys. The lanes and alleys are then numbered and the players' positions correspond with them.

Player 1 has middle-lane responsibility, players 2 and 3 are responsible for the right and left lanes respectively and the 4 man fills either the right or left alley with the 5 man trailing. None of the players change positions without directives from the coach. This eliminates confusion in the break. You want all of the spots filled with the proper people executing their responsibilities. Diagram 7-1 shows the full court divided into lanes and alleys.

Once you have divided the court and labeled the areas, you divide the back-court into three outlet areas. There is plenty of operating room for player 1 to start the break once he receives the outlet pass. (Diagram 7-2)

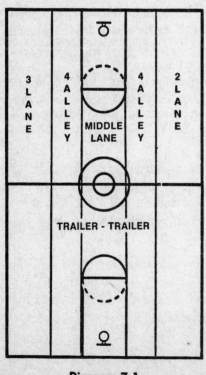

Diagram 7-1

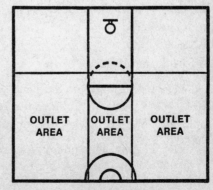

Diagram 7-2

Starting the Controlled Fast Break

In starting the fast break, it is important to have all the players think "fast break" in the sense of making a quick transition from defense to offense. Playing a pressure man-for-man defense is instrumental to starting a quick fast break. With all the players playing tough, aggressive defense, their mental and physical transition into the fast break should be instantaneous.

The defensive rebound is the most common way to start the fast break, with its success depending on how quickly the outlet can be made. Our defensive rebounders are instructed to shout "ball" when they obtain the missed shot. Upon hearing this, the other four men can assume their fast-break duties immediately.

When the rebounder obtains the ball, he should protect it by placing it over his head or under his chin with his elbows out. Coaches get gray hairs quickly when their big men get a rebound, bring it down to their waist, and then have it stripped by an alert opposing player. If this happens near the basket, it usually means two points for the opposition.

Once the rebounder has the ball, he should pivot to his outside in order to make his outlet. Ideally, you want player 1 to receive the outlet pass all the time. He must position himself on the side of rebound and as deep down-court as possible. He must signal the rebounder when he is clear by shouting "1 man." If they can get the ball to player 1 without having to go to a secondary receiver, they can start the break that much faster.

Once player 1 has the ball, he should maintain control with his dribble to half-court. He must then make a decision as to whether he has an advantage situation or not. If he passes to one of the wings, the pass should lead to a score. If he elects to keep the ball and take it to the foul-line area, he has several options to choose from. Player 1 can stop at the line and shoot the 15-foot jumper if the defense sags on the wings. If the defense picks him up, he can pass to one of his wing men who are cutting on the blocks. Also, he can clear his dribble and look for the trailer or he can pull the ball out and get into a half-court offense. The options that player 1 chooses from are dictated by what the defense does.

Fast Break Factors

Before describing the personnel requirements for the Controlled Fast Break, there are some fast break factors that must be introduced to and understood by your players.

1) Player 1 must go to the side of the rebound and call "1 Man." This will alert the rebounder to where he is.

2) The ball should be outletted to player 1· if possible.

3) Player 1 must go as deep down-court as possible to receive the outlet pass.

4) If player 1 is covered, players 2 and 3, when sprinting to their spots, must come back as secondary receivers, and then the player who receives passes to player 1 or switches with player 1 to start the break.

5) If player 1 is overplayed, he must move to an open spot and come back for the ball.

6) Player 1 always goes to the side to where he has advanced the ball.

7) Players 2 and 3 stay even with player 1 in an advantage situation, and cut in on the blocks after using a change-of-direction move from about the free-throw line extended.

8) All rebounders, after coming down, must pivot outside and protect the ball by holding it under their chin or over their head.

9) All rebounders, after securing the rebound, must establish a wide base.

10) All rebounders must signal "ball" when the rebound has been secured.

11) All rebounders should use the over-the-head pass, two-hand chest pass, hook or baseball pass when outletting the ball.

12) All rebounders should only dribble to escape trouble or to get a better passing angle.

13) Players 4 and 5 must shuffle-slide from the foul line inward. This footwork assures better body balance and control. It is also easier to catch a pass from the corner if the player is facing the ball.

14) Upon receipt of an advancing pass in the break, that player must pivot and read the situation before making any kind of move. This pivot will enable him to see any offensive player ahead and it will reduce the possibility of the offensive foul.

Personnel Requirements

In organizing the fast break, you should number each player by the position you want him to maintain in your fast break alignment.

Player 1   —usually the point guard in your offense and the middle man in the fast break. He is your best ballhandler, and must be equal with his ballhandling ability in going in either direction.

He must possess a keen knowledge of the game and be an excellent passer.

Player 2   —the right-side wing man, who must be an adequate ball-handler and a good jump shooter from the 12 to 15-foot range. He is usually the other guard.

Player 3   —the left-side wing man. He is your quicker, smaller forward, who must be an adequate ballhandler and a good jump-shooter from the 12 to 15-foot range.

Player 4   —the center, who must possess good hands and strong power-moves from the low-post area.

Player 5   —the trailer or safety man. He is your bigger, less mobile forward, who must possess good shooting ability from the top of the key. He will have many shots from the key area in the swing series.

Advantage Situation

An advantage situation occurs when you have more offensive men than defensive men down-court in the transition game. Player 1 will look for an opening down the middle of the floor for the outlet. If the rebounder is unable to hit Player 1 with the outlet, he can pass to 2 or 3 from the foul line to half-court, and that player will in turn hit player 1 in the middle of the floor.

In quick-outlet situations where the rebounder can hit player 1 directly, the options are:

1)   Player 1 can hit player 2 or 3 in the layup position with a lob-pass over the defense. (Diagram 7-3)

2)   Players 2 and 3 can read that it is an advantage situation and wait for player 1 to advance with his dribble, staying even with him until they reach the foul-line extended. At this point, players 2 and 3 use a change-of-direction move and cut to the goal. (Diagram 7-4)

3)   Players 2 and 3 stay wide and allow player 1 to penetrate to the basket. This will allow player 1 to dish off to either 2 or 3 if the defense collapses on the penetration move. (Diagram 7-5)

4)   When players 2 and 3 stay wide, player 4 hustles down the floor, looking for daylight as the defense spreads to cover the wings. Player 4 can then receive a lob-pass from player 1 down the middle or on either side of the free-throw lane. (Diagram 7-6)

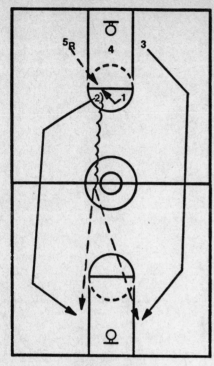

Diagram 7-3

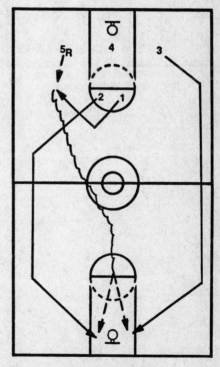

Diagram 7-4

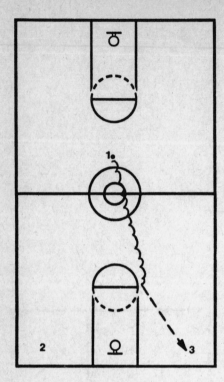

Diagram 7-5

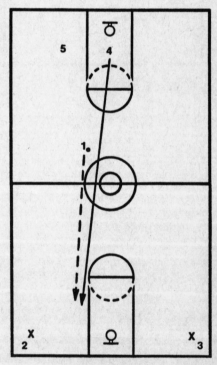

Diagram 7-6

Non-Advantage Situation

In a non-advantage situation, you should advance the ball to the corners to either player 2 or 3, depending on who is open for the down-court pass. It is very important that player 1 "reads" the defensive situation instantly and makes the correct decision on whether you are in an advantage situation or in a non-advantage situation.

In the non-advantage situation, player 1 will execute a lob-pass to either player 2 or 3 in the right or left corner. The player who sprints to the corner and receives this lob-pass must do so with a jump-stop. The lob-pass, coupled with the jump-stop will enable the wing man to maintain better body control in performing this maneuver. Many fast break opportunities are spoiled if the ball is "fired" on a line to the sprinting players. Sometimes this pass is mishandled, thrown away or results in some other turnover. The lob gets over the defense, is a softer pass and minimizes turnovers.

When the wing men receive the down-court pass from player 1, they should look for the following options:

1) Cheat in and look for the jump-shot.
2) Stay wide and keep the middle open for penetration.
3) Look to pass back to the 1 Man.
4) Look to the alley.

Alley

If no shot is taken by either player 2 or 3, player 4 will fill what we refer to as the alley. The alley (approximately ten feet wide of the key, right or left) to be filled is determined by which side player 1 passed the ball to. If player 2 has the ball, the alley to be filled is on the right side and if player 3 has the ball, the alley is on the left side.

Player 4 should shuffle-slide facing the ball and receive a bounce-pass in the layup position. The bounce-pass is easier to handle while moving and the sliding helps the player maintain better body balance as he tries to execute a power-move in close.

Player 1 will always go to the side where he advanced the ball and look for the following options:

1) Cheat in for a shot if the alley is not available.
2) Stay back and be ready to swing the ball to the weak side. (Diagram 7-7)

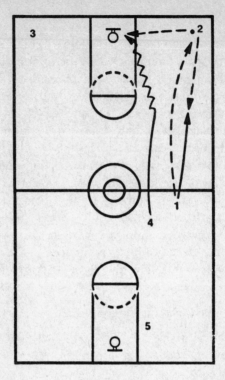

Diagram 7-7

Swing-Pass Series

If none of the previously mentioned options produce a scoring opportunity, you should then try to swing the ball to the weakside and look for other shooting or penetrating maneuvers. Quickly review the player positioning by looking at Diagram 7-8.

Player 5 trails the break. Since he is a good outside shooter, he should step *into* the key area and look for the jumper at the top of the key, or he could swing the ball to player 2 or 3 if they are open for a shot.

Diagram 7-9 illustrates the play if player 5 has swung the ball to player 3. Player 3 must use the same options that were available to player 2. These options are:

1) Cheat in for a shot.
2) Stay wide in order to open up the middle for penetration.

If player 3 stays wide, player 4 (on the opposite side of the key) moves to the ball, looking for a pass from 3 and a power-move inside.

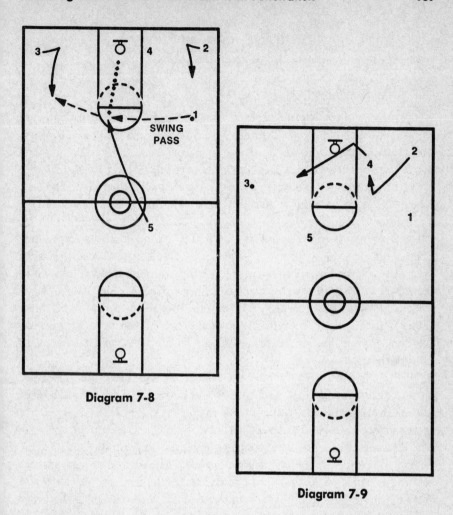

SWING
PASS

Diagram 7-8

Diagram 7-9

At any point during these maneuvers, the player with the ball can penetrate with a drive to the basket. However, in order to eliminate defensive help, player 4 must clear out to permit this drive.

A big advantage of using this Controlled-Fast Break is that there is a smooth transition into any of the multiple penetrating half-court offensive attacks. This is especially true when you are running the 1-3-1 Passing-Game Offense. If you haven't scored after the break is completed, you are ready in your half-court offensive attack.

Many coaches order offense back out to "set up" if they don't score off the fast break. You shouldn't do this, because it provides the defense with time to regroup and pick up on their defensive assignments.

Drills for Developing the
Controlled Fast Break

Fast-Break Progression Drill

You should stress fundamentals, with certain fundamentals being given emphasis on each given day. Diagram 7-10 illustrates the Fast-Break Progression Drill. All the players are lined up in two lines as seen in the diagram. One player steps out near the foul line and becomes the first player 1. Two balls are used with the first two players in line 1 having them. The first player in line 1 tosses the ball off the board and outlets to the first player 1, who uses a change-of-direction move before taking the pass. Meanwhile, the first player in line 2 sprints down the right side with his right hand raised as a target and, after using a change-of-direction move near the foul-line extended, heads for the basket. Player 1 takes several dribbles, jump-stops and throws a lob-pass to the player cutting in towards the basket from the right side in the layup position. Player 1 trails the play, rebounds the shot and outlets to the shooter. Player 1 then sprints down the right side, with the shooter taking several dribbles, jump-stops and makes a lob-pass to player 1, who is cutting in towards the goal.

After the first shot, the next players step up and repeat the procedure. You should execute the drill with both balls at both ends of the court. The drill can be run the next day from the left side so that the players have equal practice time with both hands. The players, of course, switch lines after each trip.

The next phase of the progression series is executed just like the first drill, except that player 2, sprinting down-court, sees he has no advantage. Instead of using a change-of-direction move to the basket, he heads for the corner and receives the lob-pass from player 1 and takes a 12 to 15-foot jump-shot from the corner. Player 1 rebounds and outlets to player 2. Then he sprints down-court, receives the lob pass in the corner and takes the 12 to 15-foot jump-shot. Meanwhile, the next players in their respective lines are continuing the drill, beginning when the first shot was taken. The players switch lines. (Diagram 7-11)

Three-Man Progression Drill

The Three-Man Progression Drill starts just like the previous progression drills. The rebounder outlets to player 1 who then passes to player 2 who is sprinting to the corner. The rebounder, however, sprints down the court and shuffle-slides into the right alley, facing the ball (which is in the corner) and receives a bounce-pass from player 2. He now executes a power-move to the

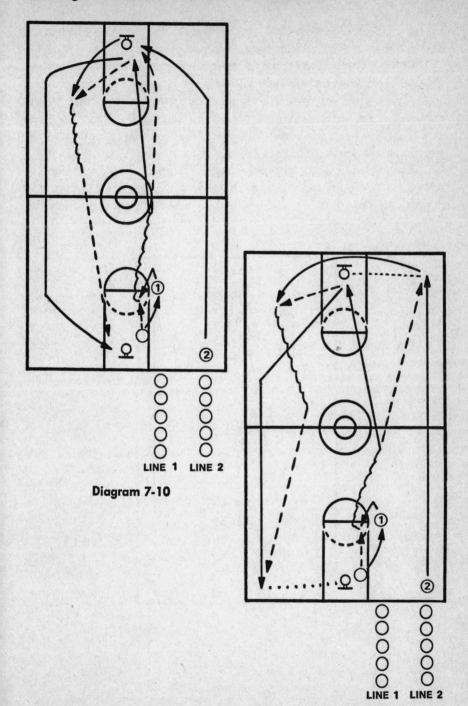

LINE 1   LINE 2

Diagram 7-10

LINE 1   LINE 2

Diagram 7-11

basket. Remember that the outside man, player 2 or 3, must stay wide and use a bounce-pass, which is easier to handle while on the move.

Player 1 rebounds the shot and outlets to player 2, who has now become the new player 1 on the trip back. The original rebounder becomes player 2 and player 1 slides in for the power-shot. The next group of three players continues the drill, beginning after the first shot is taken. You must stress timing in all of the fast-break drills, and all of the players must read the situation so that they aren't moving too fast or too slow. (Diagram 7-12)

You should then take these drills and reverse them to player 3's side, the left side of the court. Always have your players use right-hand dribbles and power-shots on player 2's side or right side and left-hand dribbles and power-shots on player 3's side.

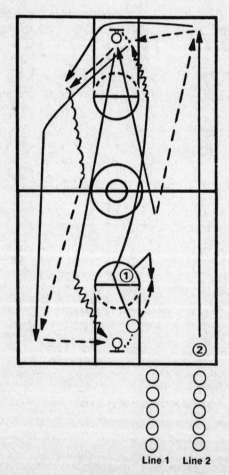

Line 1　　Line 2

Diagram 7-12

Four-Man Series

Diagram 7-13 illustrates the Four-Man Series. Unlike the previous progression drills, you use only one ball in this drill. Four players are placed at one end of the court, with the rest of the team at the other end. The drill starts with four players stepping on to the court and assuming the roles of players 1, 2, 3 and the trailer or player 5. Player 5 tosses the ball off the board and outlets to player 1. Players 2 and 3 sprint down their respective sides. Player 1 takes several dribbles, jump-stops and hits player 2 with a lob-pass in the corner. He then follows that pass for a return pass and the swing series. Player 5 trails the play and sets up at the top of the key. At this point, you should tell your players what option to use on the swing pass. A good way to keep your players alert is to have them shoot on your whistle. Remember to stress timing and change-of-direction moves. After the first group is completed, the four players who were down at the far end continue the drill by heading down-court and executing in the same manner.

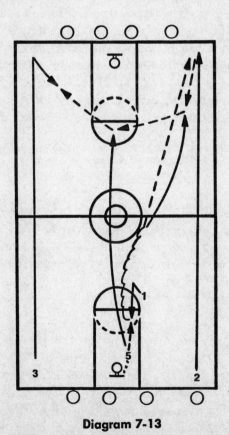

Diagram 7-13

Five-Man Fast Break

The last phase of the Controlled Fast Break is illustrated in Diagram 7-14. It is a five-man drill that incorporates all of the previously mentioned progression maneuvers.

One ball is used in this drill, and five players start it by assuming all the positions in the Controlled Fast Break. The remaining players wait their turn at the opposite end of the court.

Player 5 outlets the ball to player 1, who takes several dribbles and looks for either player 2 or 3. For the purpose of the drill, you should have your men continue to pass to the 2 Man. When player 1 passes deep to player 2, he follows his pass. Player 4 hustles down-court and fills the right alley, shuffling in as he hits his area. After player 5 completes his outlet, he sprints to the top of the key, looking for the swing series.

If player 2 cannot shoot, he passes back to player 1, who looks for the shot or a penetrating move. If these options are unavailable, player 1 swings the ball to player 5 at the top of key, who looks for his shot or penetration move. Meanwhile, player 3 gets rid of his man with a change-of-direction move and comes to the ball. After shuffling in, player 4 jumps into the lane or opposite low post, looking for a pass in deep for his power-move.

These are the options in the Controlled Fast Break. They can be mirrored on the opposite side of the court, which provides you with an explosive multiple-option Controlled Fast Break. Player 1 is the key, because he must be able to instantly read the situation ahead and decide what to do with the ball.

Fundamental Drills for the
Controlled Fast Break

All of the passing, dribbling and moves drills illustrated in this and other chapters are essential for the development of the Controlled Fast Break. However, the following fundamental drills are used as individual and team oriented drills that aid in the execution and development of the Controlled Fast Break.

Drill for Player 1

One of the prerequisites for a solid player in the guard position is that he be able to advance the ball under defensive pressure. The Drill for Player 1 helps him develop the necessary skill and poise needed to defeat pressure defenses.

Diagram 7-15 illustrates the setup for the Drill for Player 1. The court is divided lengthwise into three lanes. Three players start the drill at one end in

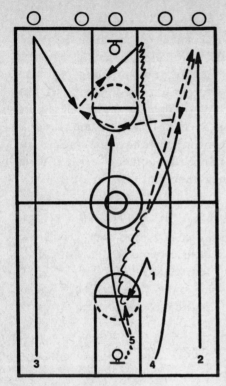

Diagram 7-14

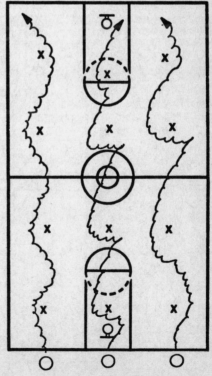

Diagram 7-15

their respective lanes, each possessing a ball. The rest of the squad is stationed in the lanes as defenders and are spread out at random or equal distances apart.

On your whistle, the three players start dribbling toward the defenders while staying in their own lanes. The defenders are instructed to offer more than a token effort in trying to deflect, steal or cause the dribbler to lose the ball. If the dribbler is successful in reaching the opposite end without losing the ball, he is through. If he loses the ball, he starts over, continuing the drill until he is successful in reaching the other end. As each player completes his turn, he takes his turn on defense and a defender becomes player 1. Remind your players to keep their heads up while dribbling.

Three-on-Two, Two-on-One Drill

In this drill, we are working with a three-on-two advantage fast break situation, coupled with a two-on-one advantage situation coming back. This is also a good defensive drill against the fast break.

Diagram 7-16 illustrates the execution of the Three-on-Two, Two-on-One Drill. The ball is outletted to player 1 with the wings staying even with

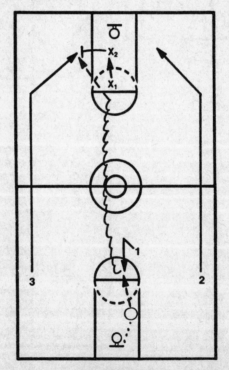

Diagram 7-16

the ball. As they proceed down court and approach the foul-line extended, the wings cut in on the blocks, looking for the ball. X1 is responsible for the ball with X2 taking the first pass and X1 dropping in to protect the basket.

Diagram 7-17 shows the second phase of this drill. The two players who were on defense rebound the shot and *must* pass back and forth up the court. The first player who outletted the ball is now the lone defender against the two new attackers. As soon as the attackers reach the foul line area, they are instructed to take the ball to the basket. Another pass here could result in a deflection, steal or some other turnover.

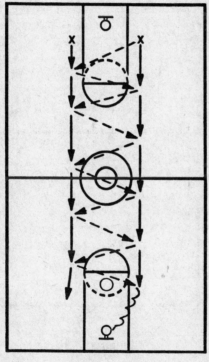

Diagram 7-17

Round-Robin Drill

The Round-Robin Drill shown in Diagram 7-18 is designed to coach offensive players on how to move to the ball, as well as teaching the baseball and overhead passes. The squad is divided into four groups, facing in from the sidelines. There is a player at each baseline with a ball. On your whistle, the first four players use change-of-direction moves away from the ball in their half of the court and then come back to receive the pass. The first pass is a baseball pass. The receiver takes the ball with a jump-stop, pivots outside and makes a two hand overhead pass to the player ahead of him. The second player now takes the ball to the basket with a hard dribble. This action takes place simultaneously on both sidelines and baselines. Players rotate counter-clockwise.

Diagram 7-18

Head-Pass Drill

The Head-Pass Drill shown in Diagram 7-19, is an excellent drill for coaching how to pass on the move, and it helps in the development of peripheral vision. The players line up as shown, with the first two players stepping out as passers. One player has a ball and starts the drill with a pass, and then the players continue down and back, passing the ball back and forth. Upon each reception, the players must look up before passing. This will aid the players in learning to look before they start to move with the ball, and it helps to eliminate the offensive foul. This drill can also be executed with three players and two balls.

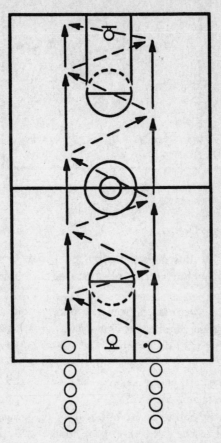

Diagram 7-19

Change-of-Direction Drill

The Change-of-Direction Drill is used to coach players on how to go backdoor off the fast break. We are usually in our half-court offense at the completion of the break, and the backdoor is an excellent move to use when the defense isn't quite set. Some teams try to overplay the swing series, which makes them vulnerable to a backdoor move. (Diagram 7-20) The squad is divided into two groups. The players at the right execute a Z-cut, planting the left foot and with the left arm extended as a decoy, cut sharply to the basket. After taking the pass, they first make a layup and then make a jump-shot. Players rotate lines.

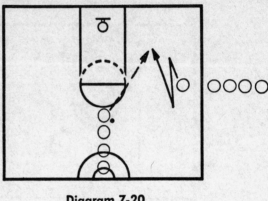

Diagram 7-20

11-Man Continuity Drill

Diagram 7-21 illustrates the popular 11-Man Continuity Drill. This drill touches on many fundamentals like passing, dribbling, shooting, timing and conditioning.

In this drill, eleven players are used at once. If you have more than eleven players, just rotate the number necessary to include the extra men. The drill is started with players 1, 2 and 3 bringing the ball down the court with the 1 Man in possession. Players X_1 and X_2 are in their fast-break defensive positions. Player X_1 takes the ball, player X_2 takes the first pass and X_1 sags opposite. As soon as the shot is taken, players 1, 2, 3, X_1 and X_2 rebound. The player who rebounds outlets the ball to either 4 or 5. If X_1 rebounds, he joins 4 and 5 in bringing the ball to the other end of the court.

Players X_2, 1, 2 and 3 fill the other spots; two as outlet men and two in the defensive positions. This drill can be executed for as long as you like. It is best to stress a different fundamental each time the drill is used.

These are the basic drills used to develop the Controlled Fast Break with the Progression Series being the bread-and-butter drills. These drills were designed to favor control of the situation at hand.

The fast break is the first offensive option. It should be under control in order to produce scoring potential that puts pressure on the defense. Because it is a controlled break, you must remind your players that discipline and patience are extremely important. The players must learn to develop a strategic attitude about the Controlled Fast Break, recognize advantage and non-advantage situations and when the fast break should be carried to its final option.

The players must further understand that the fast break is an explosive offensive weapon that can be used, but not abused. That is, it should be used in its rightful place and with proper execution. To run helter-skelter will produce nothing but wasted energy. The Controlled Fast Break has the advantage over the defense. It will add pressure and produce penetration and the high-percentage shot if played with patience, discipline and control.

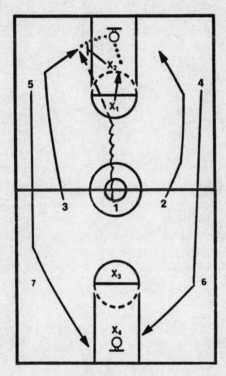

Diagram 7-21

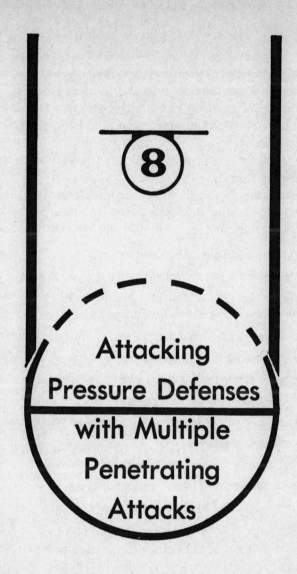

8

Attacking Pressure Defenses with Multiple Penetrating Attacks

The Use of Pressure Defenses

Pressure defenses of the past were normally used by teams who were trailing with just a few minutes remaining to play. These pressure tactics were an attempt to try to score quickly, while upsetting the opposition's offensive tempo.

Today, variations of pressure defenses are increasingly becoming the basic defensive ploy for many teams. As a result, they are sometimes used from the opening tip to the final buzzer.

With the proficient offenses of players, the defense must use tactics that attempt to disrupt the normal and free-lance movement of the players and which ultimately attack the offensive tempo itself. Pressure defenses attempt to spread the offense, thus reducing its effectiveness. However, if teams are prepared to meet and counter the various man-for-man, zone, combinations, run-and-jump, half-court, three-quarter court and full-court presses, then the defense's intentions can be negated.

Using pressure defensive tactics will help you understand the strengths and weaknesses of the press. This understanding will aid you in developing confidence when preparing against the pressure defense. To understand some of the reasons why pressure defenses are used, you must look at some of the more common stratagems of pressure defenses. Pressure defenses:

- Upset the normal offensive movement.
- Try to physically and mentally wear the opposition down.
- Strive to keep the opposition's big men away from the basket by making them come out to handle the ball.
- Cause turnovers by teams that are weak in their fundamentals.
- Disrupt ball control or patterned teams.
- Attempt to change and control game tempo.
- May cause teams to lose their poise.
- Are used by small, quick teams to negate height disadvantages.
- Are offenses themselves.
- Force hurried and poor-percentage shots.
- Usually require sound strategy to be beaten.
- Place the opposition into double-team situations.

Psychological Outlook Against
the Press

There is a tendency, especially with young players, to panic at the first sign of a press. They become flustered and their only concern is to get rid of the ball to someone else. They forget about the ten-second rule, that the press is a gambling defense, that it is weakest in its basket coverage, that it is prone to excessive fouling and it can be exhausting. To be unprepared and to panic is to the press's liking; to commit mental and physical mistakes is to play into the hands of the pressure defense.

To combat this apparent psychological edge, we have developed anti-press principles, a simple system of guides to attacking pressure defenses. We tell our players that teams who want to press us are doing us a favor, because we know we are going to score against the press. There's nothing like stringing out several quick layups against a press. In most instances, the press will be taken off. We want our players to believe that if they are pressed, the "presser" will pay a big price.

Once our players realize that they can inbound the ball safely, get behind the defensive front line quickly, penetrate and score, then the psychological advantage that the press once enjoyed will be shifted in favor of the offense. It is this confidence, developed individually within a team concept, that shifts the psychological advantage to the offense. The wise coach will ensure this confidence by keeping his offense against the press simple. Complicated maneuvers against pressure defenses can result in total disaster for the offensive team.

Principles for Ball Advancement Versus Pressing Defenses

A set of ball advancement principles is necessary to ensure sound execution of the press attack and to develop a well-coordinated press offense. These principles, while fundamentally basic, are applicable to all types of pressure defenses and are often overlooked and taken for granted. Therefore, when practicing your press offense, constantly remind your players that it is these little things that make the total offense successful.

Ball Advancement Principles

- Divide the court lengthwise into three lanes: ball, middle and third or weakside.
- Designate one player to inbound the ball.
- Get the ball in safely.
- All players must use change-of-direction moves before coming to meet each pass.
- Bring the ball to the double-team, then pass.
- No more than two passes before half-court.
- After passing to the middle, look to the third lane.
- Beat the press in the middle.
- Keep things simple.
- Your press fast-break should be similar to your fast-break offense.
- Penetrate the defense with a numerical advantage.

- Swing the ball if penetration is unavailable.
- Each time your opponents score, assume they'll press, thus get this into your pressure-offensive alignment upon recognition of the press being deployed.
- Be aggressive to the basket and look to score. Don't be satisfied with just getting the ball over the ten-second line. Put pressure on the defense.
- You should have two guards, a forward and a big man that can handle the ball against any pressure defense.

Zone-Press Offensive Tempo

Your zone-press offensive tempo is like the multiple-offensive attacks. That is, you want to strike before the defense has a chance to form. Because zone presses try to change the offensive tempo by causing the offense to speed up, they have to be attacked with a well-coordinated plan. Certainly, one way to pull teams out of their zone press is to consistently break the press and score.

Since you are trying to score quickly against the press, it is imperative that you do score when the opportunity presents itself. Failure to score increases the effectiveness of the press.

If you are content with just getting the ball up the court in a slow-tempo attack, then you had better do so without turning the ball over and without altering your attack tempo.

Keys for Defeating Zone Presses

Before you can develop and coach any kind of press offense, you must have knowledge of the strengths and weaknesses of the press. This is especially true of zone presses. They may come in different postures such as the 1-1-2-1, 2-2-1, 3-2, 2-1-2, 1-3-1 and man-for-man with zone rotationale principles. They can appear anyplace on the court; full-, half- or three-quarter court. They can fan, float or funnel the offense, depending upon the defense's intentions. Scouting reports are very helpful in determining the posture and characteristics of the pressing defense.

In conjunction with knowledge of the pressure defense, you should also be knowledgeable in developing offensive keys to combat the threat of the zone press. The following is a list of salient keys that should be incorporated within the zone-press offense. These keys should be implemented by design and reinforced as often as necessary when practicing the zone press offense.

- The offense should try to put the ball in the middle of the court, where zone presses are most vulnerable.

- The offense should stay away from baseline corners and the immediate sidelines, as they act as extra defenders.

- Advance the ball with quick, crisp passes. Avoid the lob- and bounce-passes, which are too slow and easy to pick off.

- Do not dribble unless it is to escape trouble, or to increase a passing angle. The ball can be advanced much faster with the pass.

- Players with the ball should be alert for pressure.

- Upon receipt of passes, the players should first pivot and look up-court, always keeping the head up.

- Players should bring the ball to the double-team, then pass before the trap closes.

- Players that are double-teamed should not turn their backs to their own basket.

- Since zone presses double-team, fast break possibilities exist, and you should send your players to the goal.

- The ball should be inbounded by a designated player to avoid confusion.

- A player should always be behind the ball as a safety.

- Fast-break lanes should be filled after front-line penetration.

- All players must recognize the defense, organize and attack it with coordination, timing and confidence.

- Ball-fakes should be used to hold the defense.

- Maintain a minimum of 18-foot floor spacing. This is very important and often overlooked. Make sure your players don't bunch up.

- Don't panic and don't hurry.

- Practice is the key.

Zone-Press Offense

Basic Alignments

The most important aspect of a press offense is the execution of the press-offense alignment. Diagrams 8-1 and 8-2 illustrate the two basic press-offensive alignments that we use.

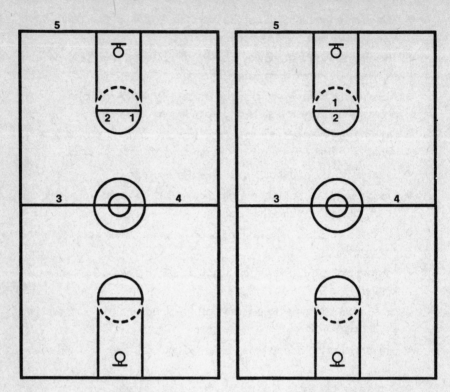

Diagram 8-1   **Diagram 8-2**

Player 5 is the player designated to inbound the ball, and he is also the safety or trailer in the press offense. You should have 5 put the ball in play because he is a post player defending near the basket and can therefore take the ball out of the net quickly and put it in play before the defense can set up against you. He is also taller than the guards who do the pressing and he can see over them. Player 1 should be your best all-around ball-handler. Player 2 is a wing guard who is a good ballhandler and passer. Player 3 is the small forward and 4 is the other post player. The responsibilities of the press-offense assignments are basically the same as in our Controlled Fast Break offense. This helps the players, because they don't have to know two separate fast-break attacks.

If you have any difficulty inbounding the ball with the alignment illustrated in Diagram 8-1, you should use the stack alignment that is seen in Diagram 8-2. This gives the defense another look and still provides you with the necessary movement and time needed to inbound the ball safely.

After your opponents have scored, you should assume that they are going to press. Therefore, you should get into your press offense alignment quickly and get the ball in safely. When 5 puts the ball in play, he is instructed to make sure he is on one side or the other of the free-throw lane. He must never get behind the basket. You should also have 5 back up one full step from the baseline to relieve himself from the pressure. When 5 puts the ball in play, he must make sure that he steps inbounds and is behind the ball.

Guard Cut

The Guard Cut is the basic maneuver used against zone pressure and can be executed from either of the two alignments. In Diagram 8-3, player 2 moves across the foul-line and screens for player 1 who uses a change-of-direction move to get open. The reason you should use a screening maneuver is that some teams use face-guarding man-for-man tactics until the ball is inbounded, after which they may use zone-press double-team tactics. The screening maneuver frees one of the guards; which one depends on which side of the lane the ball is put into play.

In Diagram 8-3, player 1 breaks to the ball from the foul-line as 2 rolls toward the ball after setting his screen. If 1 is open, he must get the ball. If he isn't open, player 2 should be open on his roll.

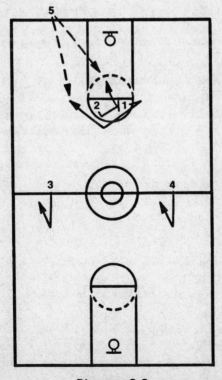

Diagram 8-3

After the ball has been successfully inbounded to one of the guards, the movement of the offense is keyed from that point. In Diagram 8-4, player 1 receives 5's inbounds pass. Have your players receive passes on their outside shoulders. This allows them to pivot away from blind-side traps. Upon pivoting, they will be able to see the entire floor before making any moves. After setting his screen, player 2 rolls towards 5 and then away from 1. This maneuver, in a man-for-man situation, would take 2's defender with him, giving 1 plenty of operating room. In the zone situation, player 1 brings the ball to the double-team, and 2 flashes into the middle on a guard-cut maneuver, looking for 1's pass. Player 5 stays behind the ball until it is advanced into the middle, then he breaks down the third lane sideline. Player 1, after passing to 2 on the guard cut, heads down the side in 2's fast-break lane. Player 3 cuts diagonally to player 3's lane and 4 fills the alley.

Teach your players that they *must read the defense* from your full-court press offense. Young players, especially, sometimes take it for granted that the passes and cutting maneuvers will be available all the time.

Weakside Flash

Diagram 8-5 illustrates 2 executing the guard-cut maneuver, but unable to receive player 1's pass. This keys the next option, The Weakside Flash. As 2 cuts down the middle, drawing the defense, player 4, seeing that 2 can't receive a pass from 1, flashes into the middle with his arm raised, presenting a target for 1. Upon receipt of this pass, player 4 pivots to the outside and looks for 5 who is open in the third lane. The position of the players is as follows: player 2, after executing the guard cut, heads for the 2-lane; player 3, after seeing 4 flash up, slides into the 3-lane; player 1, after passing to 4, cuts for the top of the key; player 4, after passing to 5 in the third lane, cuts down the middle, then slides into the fast break alley; player 5, with the ball, now hits 3 in the third lane. These angular cuts slice the defense with excellent penetration.

Pass to the Safety

If you are unable to execute the guard-cut maneuver or the weakside flash, then look to the safety man, player 5. Player 5 will lag behind the ball until he sees if the guard-cut or weakside-flash options can be executed. In Diagram 8-6, player 1, with the ball, cannot hit 2 on the guard cut or hit 4 flashing high from the weakside. Player 3 has cleared out for 2, entering into the right lane, leaving 5 as the only logical receiver left for player 1. Player 5 comes back after seeing 1 in trouble and will be open as the defense concerns itself with its double-team tactics on player 1.

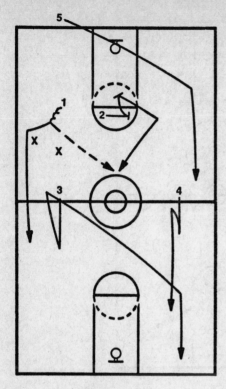

Diagram 8-4

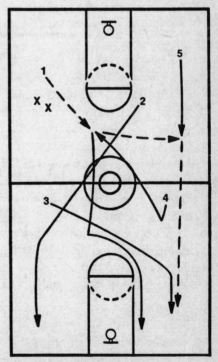

Diagram 8-5

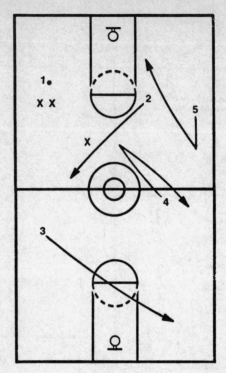

Diagram 8-6

As soon as 1 sees player 5 open, he passes the ball to him. Now, with the defense drawn away from the middle, player 1 executes a guard-cut maneuver behind the defense and receives a return pass from 5 in the middle of the defense. At this point, you should have a four-on-two advantage. The position of the players at that point is as follows: Player 1 has the ball in the middle; player 2 is in the 2 lane; player 3 is deep in the left corner; player 4 slides down the left alley and player 5 is the trailer, anticipating the next option, the swing series. (Diagram 8-7)

This press offense, with its angular cuts, in front of and behind the defense, has caused the defense to defend from sideline to sideline. This is an offensive counter that the defense does not want to face. This spreading of the defense makes it very weak both structurally and in its basket coverage.

Swing Series

The Swing Series illustrated in Diagram 8-8, is basically the same ball-reversal maneuver used in the Controlled Fast-Break Series. With the ball in the hands of player 1, in Diagram 8-7, 1 had the option of passing to player

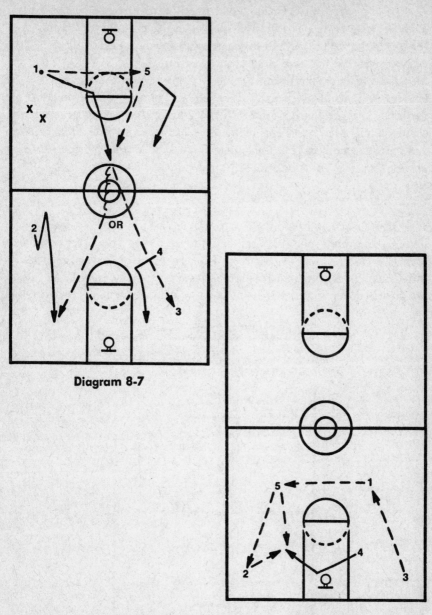

Diagram 8-7

Diagram 8-8

2 or 3. He opted for player 3 as Diagram 8-8 shows. However, you don't want to attack from the left side unless a layup is available. So far, the defense has been tilted. You should then *continue* to move the defense by swinging the ball back out and to the right side.

After player 1 hits 3 in the corner, he moves to the ball-side of the court. Player 3, after using a ball fake, passes back to player 1. Player 1 then swings the ball to the trailer, player 5 who makes a penetrating pass to player 2 in the right corner. As soon as 2 receives the pass from 5, player 4 jumps into the lane, looking for the power-move in close. Shooting options are: player 3 in the left corner; jumper by 1 cheating at the foul line; player 5 with a jumper at the top of the key; baseline drive or jumper by 2 in the right corner and the power shot by 4 in the low post. This swing series maintains excellent floor balance, spreads the defense and puts pressure on its basket coverage with penetrating moves. Yet, it still provides shooting opportunities for all the players.

Guard Cut from the Stack Alignment

The Guard-Cut from the Stack Alignment is illustrated in Diagram 8-9. On a signal from 5, both players 1 and 2 break in opposite directions to free themselves for the inbounds pass from 5. In the sequence, player 2 receives the initial pass, pivots and looks for player 1, breaking out and into the middle on the guard-cut maneuver. From this point, the entire press-offensive break is

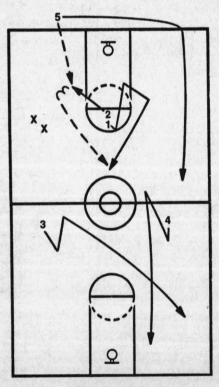

Diagram 8-9

the same as previously mentioned: player 2, after passing to 1, heads down the right side; player 3, after a change-of-direction move, slides to the left side; player 4, after his change-of-direction move, slides into the alley; player 5 lags back until he sees that 1 has gotten by the front of defense, and 1, in possession of the ball, looks for an advantage situation.

Attacking Full-Court Man-for-Man
Pressure

When faced with full-court man-for-man pressure you should work with the principle of error reduction. This is accomplished by getting the ball to your best ballhandler, player 1, clearing the court out and allowing him to work one-on-one. Once player 1 goes to work on his defender, you should adhere to the principle of 18-foot floor spacing. You don't want your players bunching up and allowing off-the-ball defensive help on your best ballhandler. Teams that like to run-and-jump or blitz-and-switch will cause serious problems if the other offensive players are too close to the dribbler.

When the other four players recognize that player 1 is working his man with the dribble, they must assume their respective floor positions in the man-for-man press offense. The key is for player 1 to recognize what kind of pressure he is confronted with. He must keep his head up in order to see the situation up-court. If he receives only token pressure, he shouldn't have any trouble penetrating. If the defense is slow in defensing or sloughing off the players in the front court, then player 1 should hit players 2 or 3 in their respective lanes.

Instruct your guards not to reverse-dribble in the middle of the floor. This is a dangerous maneuver that is susceptible to double-team tactics. If the guard is double-teamed, he should look for the other guard or for player 5, who must both recognize the situation and help out by being logical receivers. They must use change-of-direction moves to get rid of their men and come back to relieve any pressure.

Regardless of whether you are facing zone or man-for-man pressure tactics, you should attack the defense and ultimately go to the basket. Once you hit mid-court, you should get into your designated offense.

1-4 Attack Versus Man-for-Man Full-Court Pressure

When facing man-for-man full-court pressure, you should use the 1-4 alignment illustrated in Diagram 8-10. Player 5 will inbound the ball to either player 2 or player 1. Ideally, you want the ball to be in the hands of player 1.

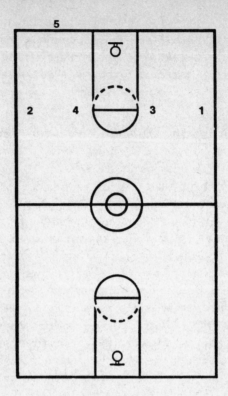

Diagram 8-10

In the diagram, player 2 is already in his lane and player 3 is only a few feet from the 3-lane. On the signal, all the players in the court use change-of-direction moves to get rid of their men. Players 1 and 2 receive rear screens to get open and, as players 3 and 4 screen for them, they roll slightly towards the ball in case the guards are not open. Remember, too, that after a basket, the player inbounding the ball can run laterally along the baseline to put the ball in play. (Diagram 8-11)

In Diagram 8-12, player 5 is successful in getting the ball to player 1. Player 5 steps inbounds and lags behind as a safety, player 3 slides down the 3 lane, player 2 heads for the 2 lane and 4 moves down court towards the alley. By these movements the offensive players are clearing out for the dribbler as they become offensive threats.

In Diagram 8-13, player 1 has successfully brought the ball near the front court. If he can beat his man, he should penetrate to the basket. If the defense converges on him, he can pass off to players 2 or 3, who are cutting to the basket.

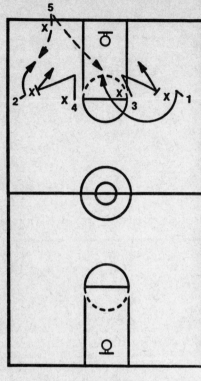

Diagram 8-11

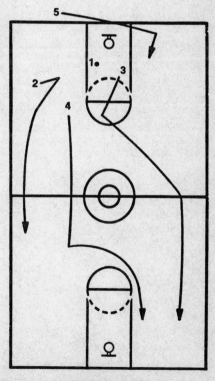

Diagram 8-12

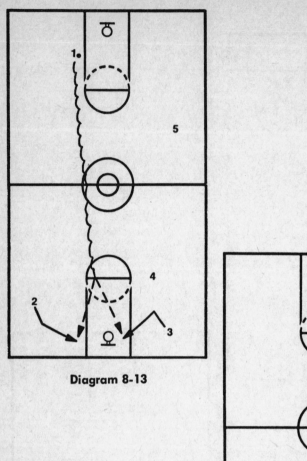

Diagram 8-13

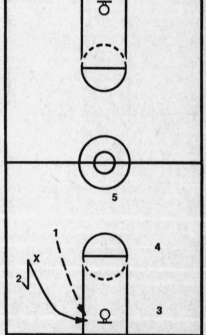

Diagram 8-14

If the full penetration is unavailable, player 1 can pass to players 2, 3 or 4 on whatever options are for the taking. For example, in Diagram 8-14 player 2's man is overplaying him, anticipating the pass from 1. Player 2, recognizing this, fakes coming to the ball, then executes a backdoor cut to the basket.

Diagram 8-15 illustrates another passing-game option. With 1 in possession of the ball, player 4 executes a down-screen on 3's defender, allowing 3 to come over the top for a medium-range jumper.

Another excellent passing-game option is a rear-screen maneuver. Diagram 8-16 shows how it is executed. With 2 getting rid of his man and coming to the ball, player 3 signals 4 by yelling "rear." He then sets a back or rear screen on 4's man, allowing 4 to cut to the basket for an uncontested layup.

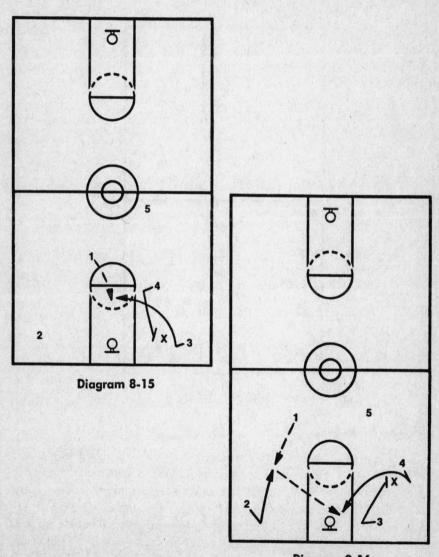

Diagram 8-15

Diagram 8-16

Swing Series

You can also execute the Swing Series from the full-court man-for-man press offense attack. In Diagram 8-17, player 1 hits 2 in the corner and moves to the ball side. Player 5 sets up at the top of the key as 4 jumps into the strongside low post. Player 2 returns the ball to 1, who swings it to 5. Player 1 or 5 can shoot or 5 can hit 3 in the left corner as 4 loops around and jumps into the opposite low post anticipating a power-move in close.

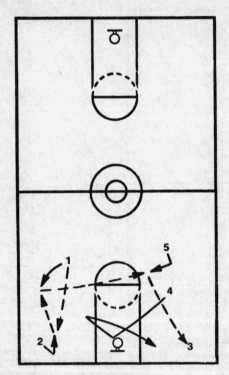

Diagram 8-17

Double-Option Bomb

If the opposition continues to defense you with their personnel between the ball and your offensive people, you should look to score quickly with the Double-Option Bomb. With all the defenders face-guarding the offense, there aren't any defenders back for basket coverage. This makes the defense extremely vulnerable to the long pass and quick-scoring layup. The baseball pass is part of our daily warmup routine and is the type of pass used in the execution of this play. Diagram 8-18 illustrates the execution of the Double-Option Bomb.

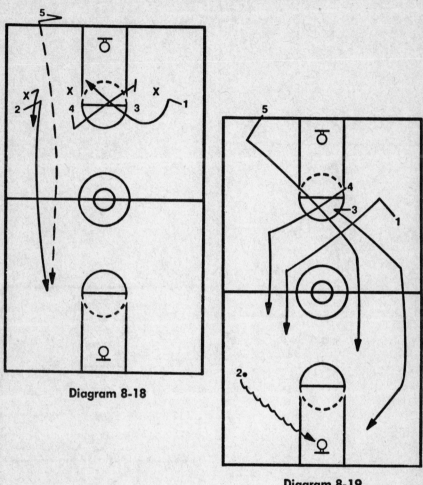

Diagram 8-18

Diagram 8-19

Player 2, instead of using a change-of-direction move away from the ball will make his move *to the ball*, then sprint down the 2-lane looking for the bomb from 5. If the pass is successfully completed, player 2 should be able to take the ball to the goal. (Diagram 8-19) Meanwhile, player 4 stacked with 3, setting up a double-screen for 1 as a safety. If 2 cannot take the ball to the goal, the players' positions are as follows: player 1 takes his position on the ball side; player 3 heads for the 3 lane; player 4 shuffle steps into the alley and 5 sets up opposite 1 anticipating the swing series. (Diagrams 8-20 and 8-21)

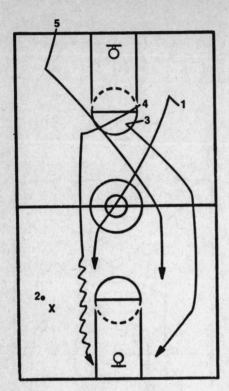

Diagram 8-20

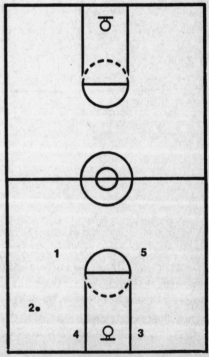

Diagram 8-21

The second option of the Double-Option Bomb is illustrated in Diagram 8-22. With player 2 down-court and unable to receive the long pass, player 1 runs his man into the double-screen set by players 3 and 4. The offensive maneuvers for the second option are as follows: player 1 has the ball and will bring it up court; simultaneously, player 3 takes several steps up court then sets a back screen on 4's defender; player 4 then cuts into the 4-alley as 3 rolls out and cuts to the 3-lane; player 5 steps in the court area behind the ball, and player 2, using a change-of-direction move, comes back toward the ball.

Diagram 8-23 illustrates the players' floor position after their cutting maneuvers.

You shouldn't use the long bomb pass too often, because doing so would reduce its effectiveness. However, when it is successful, it loosens up the defensive pressure and makes putting the ball in play a much easier task.

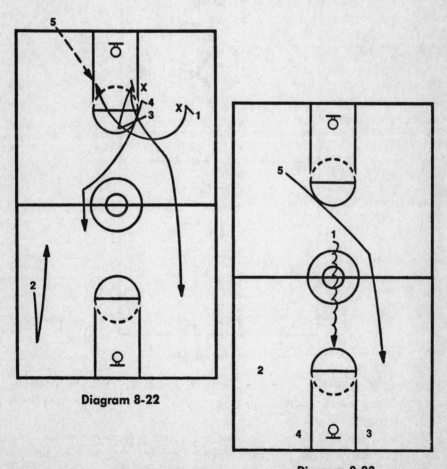

Diagram 8-22

Diagram 8-23

Attacking Half-Court Pressure

The 1-4 Versus Half-Court Man-for-Man Pressure

Most of the half-court pressure defenses are of the zone variety, but occasionally you may be faced with man-for-man half-court pressure. Regardless of the type of half-court press confronting you, you should initially deploy the high 1-4 offensive alignment. If the press is of the man-for-man variety, as illustrated in Diagram 8-24, player 1 has four entry passes to choose from with the 1-4 offensive alignment.

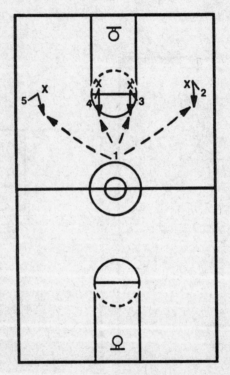

Diagram 8-24

All of the pass-receivers are in a one-on-one situation with their defenders, making it difficult for the defense to double-up on the ball. The offense must recognize the defense.

With the 1-4, any pass to either of the high-post players would key a backdoor maneuver by the wing guard on the ball side. For example, a semi-lob pass to 3 keys 2's backdoor cut to the basket as seen in Diagram 8-25.

Upon receipt of the entry pass, player 3 pivots to the basket. This always applies pressure on the defense.

Another option by 1 is to signal 2 to clear out, which would allow 1 to use a step-out screen set by 3. If 1 can penetrate all the way, he should do so. If he is stopped or if there is a defensive switch, 3 rolls to the basket. (Diagram 8-26)

From this point, if you cannot execute any of these options, you should get into your passing-game offense. Remember that this offense utilizes a lot of passing, screening and movement; fundamentals that a pressing defense doesn't want to see.

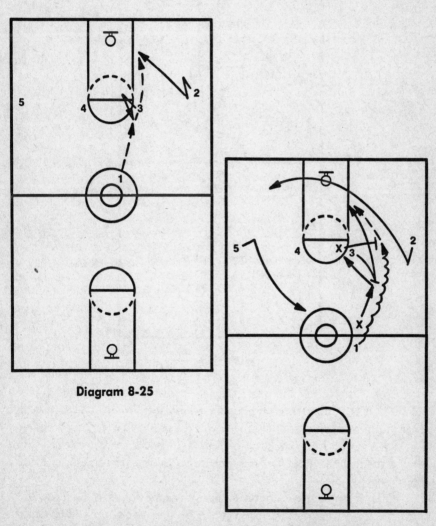

Diagram 8-25

Diagram 8-26

The 1-4 Versus Half-Court Zone Pressure

When faced with a zone half-court press (the 1-3-1 and 1-2-2 are two of the more popular types) you should again use the high 1-4 zone attack. To maintain floor balance and organization, you must attack the half-court zone press with short, quick, crisp right-angle passing, coupled with player movement. Diagram 8-27 shows the 1-4 attack versus a 1-3-1 half-court trapping defense.

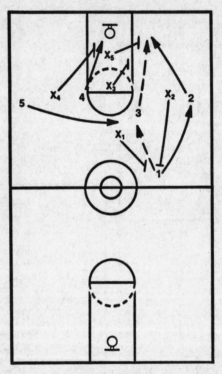

Diagram 8-27

As X₁ and X₂ jump player 1, he hits 3 who comes out and relieves the pressure. When 2 sees X₂ trapping, he slides to the right low post with 1 replacing him in the wing and 5 moving to the point. Player 3 pivots and hits 2 low. If 2 had gone to the deep corner, X₅ would have had to check him, leaving the low post open for 3 to slide into. This move enables 2 to make a return-pass in close.

If player 2 cannot execute any of his options, he returns the ball to 1, who can hit 3 in the high post. Player 3 can shoot or pass to 5 at the point. Player 5 can shoot or hit 4 who comes out on the left side. Meanwhile, player 2 moved along the baseline, anticipating the ball reversal and the baseline series option. (Diagram 8-28)

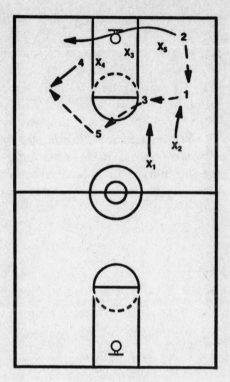

Diagram 8-28

If you know your opponents will press you at half-court, you should adhere to the controlled fast-break principles. You want to beat the defense from foul-line to foul-line with penetration. Because the half-court press is an extension of a team's basic defense being deployed, you won't practice a great deal against half-court pressure unless your opponents have an exceptional press with exceptional personnel. To dwell on an opponent's press may constitute a lack of confidence in your ability to break it in the minds of your players.

The full-court press offense is an extension of your controlled fast break and your half-court press attack incorporates one of your multiple penetrating attacks. Through repetitive practicing, you can develop the coordination and poise needed to defeat pressure defenses. Along with the use of your press-offense principles, your players must learn to recognize the defense, develop the necessary court savvy needed to make the right decision and learn to take advantage of opportunistic situations. You should introduce your press offensive philosophy early, have patience and build confidence within your team. With a sound system of attack, one that is adaptable to different defensive tactics, the offense will remain confident in its execution and will exert pressure on the presser.

In preparing for the press, break down your whole offensive scheme into parts. Take all of the movements and use breakdown drills to coordinate your attack. For example, work on the guards freeing themselves to receive the inbounds pass. Then, concentrate on the guard cut. Then, execute the offense without the guard cut, forcing the weakside-flash option to be used. Next, concentrate on hitting the third lane and having the players fill their respective fast-break positions. Concentrate on cutting, screening, passing and moving without the ball, or getting into your half-court offense. Work one-on-one and on your backdoor cuts. Through this, you will develop poise and confidence in defeating the pressure defenses.

9

Special Situation Plays with Multiple Penetrating Attacks

Scoring Plays From Out-of-Bounds

While it is generally accepted that putting the ball in play is the most important phase of an out-of-bounds situation, you have to go one step further—you have to try to score.

Your philosophy in execution should be to provide plays that work against both the man-for-man and zone defenses and are similar to each other regardless of formation. In addition, they should provide scoring possibilities for the player who inbounds the ball. This player is the least guarded, and if he is a good shooter, he can take advantage of defensive lapses.

Since most teams having out-of-bounds plays utilize them against man-for-man defenses, I will only illustrate the zone situations on under-the-basket situations, because the plays can be executed against man-for-man and zone defenses.

Player Positions

You should have your players maintain relative positions in all of your plays. This eliminates confusion and insures sound execution. Here is a key to the players in the following diagrams

- Player 1 will be the point guard.
- Players 2 and 5 are the wing guards.
- Players 3 and 4 are the post men.

Players 3 and 4 can be a post man and a forward or two post men or two forwards.

Horizontal

This play was designed to combat the zone defenses, but it will work against the man-for-man defense as well. As shown in Diagram 9-1, player 2 is inbounding the ball to player 1, who (with player 5) fakes toward the ball, then moves out. Meanwhile, players 3 and 4 are setting a double-screen along the free-throw lane opposite the side where the ball is put in play.

Diagram 9-2 shows 1 reversing the ball to player 5, who now looks for 2 coming behind the two-man screen. Player 2 can shoot, or if one of the

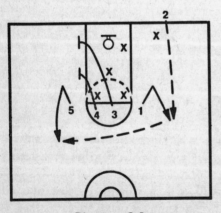

Diagram 9-1

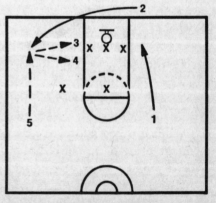

Diagram 9-2

defensive players breaks the screen, he can "jam-it" into 3 or 4 for the close-in power-shot. Notice that player 1 moves down for offensive rebounding on the weakside and either 3 or 4 (depending upon which player is not a logical receiver) has strongside rebound responsibility. Player 5 remains back for defense.

Stack

The Stack play (Diagram 9-3) positions the players in a double-stack alignment. You should always place the two biggest players closest to the ball with the two best shooters behind them. In addition, the number 2 man is always stacked on the side of the ball in this play, so he can get the quick jump shot.

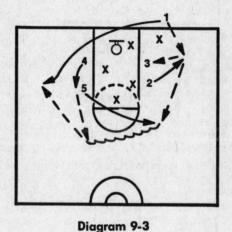

Diagram 9-3

Player 1 inbounds the ball to 2, who looks for the quick jump shot or possible pass in close to 3 for his power-move to the basket. If these options are unavailable, player 2 looks for 5, who has moved to the top of the key. Upon receipt of this pass, player 5 moves quickly to his left and hits 1 coming off the screen set by 4, or he can hit 4 who has "exploded" to the ball after 1 goes by. If a defensive man breaks 4's screen, player 1 should be alert for 4, who may be open for a close-in power-move. Player 5 is back for defensive balance. Players 3 and 4 are in excellent offensive rebounding position, with player 2 assuming middle-rebounding duties if the ball is reversed.

Vertical

In the Verticle play (Diagram 9-4), player 1 inbounds the ball to 2, who looks for the quick jump-shot. If this option fails to materialize, player 2 can "jam-it" to 3, who has already posted up. Player 4, meanwhile, clears to the opposite side and sets a screen for 1.

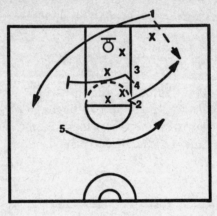

Diagram 9-4

Diagram 9-5 shows a situation in which 2 could not shoot or hit 3 low. He passes the ball to 5, who dribbles to his left and looks for 1 coming off the screen set by 4. Or, he can push the ball into 4 low if the defensive player breaks 4's screen. This play is especially effective because, regardless of the shot's location, there is a big man in offensive rebounding position. Players 1 and 2 assume middle-rebound responsibility and 5 stays back for defense.

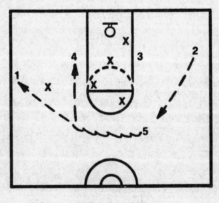

Diagram 9-5

Box

The box formation isn't new, but it isn't often used against teams that zone out-of-bounds situations. In Diagram 9-6, player 3 initiates the play by executing a simple pick-and-roll with 2. Player 2 looks for the quick jumper or the pass into 3 and his power-move to the basket.

If these two options fail to develop, player 2 looks back to 5, who has moved to his right as a safety valve. Player 5 (Diagram 9-7) reverses the ball and looks for 1 coming behind 4, or he hits 4 low for the high-percentage shot. Player 2 has middle-rebound responsibilities, players 3 and 4 remain low and 5 stays back for defense.

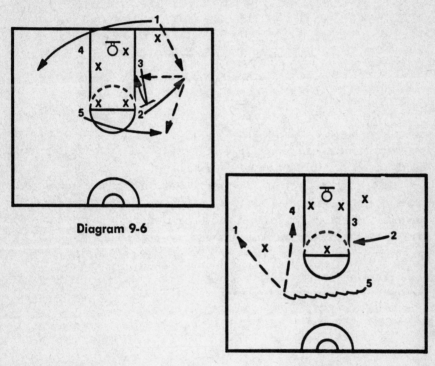

Diagram 9-6

Diagram 9-7

A Successful Side-Out Series

Four-Option Continuity Play. The Side-Out series maintains the basic philosophy of simple execution and providing scoring opportunities for the player who inbounds the ball. This play has four options.

In Diagram 9-8, player 1 inbounds the ball to 2, whose man is screened by 5. If there is room to penetrate, player 2 should take the ball in for the layup. If either 3 or 4's defensive man picks up 2, he can pass to the open man for another close-in shot. Players 3 and 4, who are stacked, should face the ball. This is necessary for a reverse-pivot and solid screen to be set on 1's man in the next option.

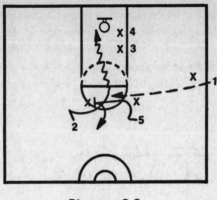

Diagram 9-8

In Diagram 9-9, assume that 2 cannot drive to the basket. Maintaining his dribble, player 1 takes his man deep, then swings back out and takes the pass from 2 for the short jumper. It is vital that 4 set a solid screen by pivoting on his *left* foot so that he can locate 1's defender.

Diagram 9-10 illustrates the third and fourth options of the Side-Out series. Player 1 again inbounds to 2, but instead of going low, he swings around the double-screen set by 3 and 4. He then takes the pass and shoots from inside the free-throw lane. If 1 is not open, player 4 moves around a pick set by 3 and looks for the pass from 2 for the close-in shot.

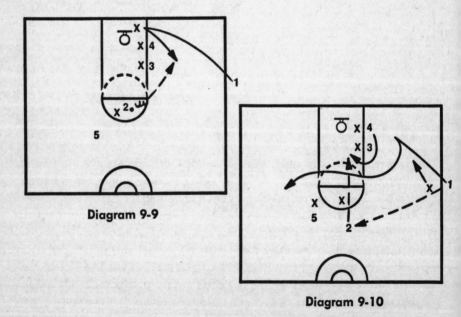

Diagram 9-9

Diagram 9-10

<u>Half-Court Last-Second Shot.</u> Trying not to leave any stones un-
turned, you should diligently practice last-second shots from the half-court
and full-court areas.

Diagram 9-11 illustrates our half-court play. Wing guard 5 executes a
"V" pattern in and out and receives a pass from 2, your best shooter. Player 3
immediately sets a screen for 2, who can choose to go over-the-top or take the
low route, looking for the pass from 5 and the shot. Note that you have players
1 and 4 set up wide of the free-throw lane. They entertain their defensive men
and, at the same time, allow player 2 plenty of operating room.

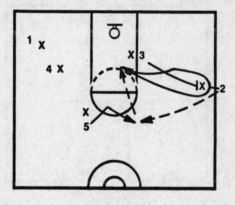

Diagram 9-11

Full-Court Last-Second Shot Versus
Man-for-Man Pressure

The Home Run

In this situation (Diagram 9-12), your opponents have scored and are
applying man-for-man pressure. You react by having players 3, 4 and 5 form a
triple-screen for player 2 on the strong side, about twelve feet from the end
line. Meanwhile, player 1, who is the best ballhandler, sets up on the
weakside. As soon as 2 is set to inbound the ball, player 1 jumps out-of-bounds
and takes a pass from player 2. Player 2 then runs his man into the three-man
screen and takes a long pass on the fly from 1.

The clock doesn't start until the ball is touched by a player who is in
bounds. Therefore, the lateral pass from 2 to 1 doesn't waste valuable time,
because passing is the quickest way of advancing the ball. Therefore, in this
type of full-court play where time is such a critical factor, dribbling should be
discouraged unless absolutely necessary.

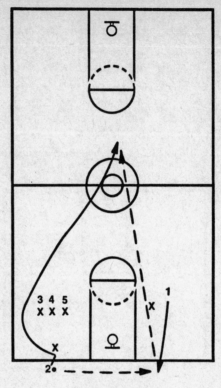

Diagram 9-12

Practice Organization

Out-of-bounds scoring plays which are fundamentally sound and easy to execute can add to the potency of your offense. When there are out-of-bounds situations, the defense, sometimes has a tendency to relax, making it more vulnerable to quick scoring. Practice is the key to success. Devoting five or ten minutes of a regular practice session to special-situation plays can be the difference between winning and losing.

The Special

The Special is a clear-out play for player 2. The situation usually calls for a quick basket or the loosening of the defense if you are being given some pressure.

The Special is signaled from the bench and the players align as seen in Diagram 9-13. The play starts with player 1 passing to 2 and moving behind him for a handoff. After the exchange, player 2 rubs his man off a high screen set by player 3. Player 1 must lob the ball to 2 in the layup position. If 4's defensive man switches, player 1 hits 4 low and has an easy layup. This play works well because there is no weakside defensive help to stop it. (Diagram 9-14)

The 2 man does not need to be a big player or leaper. Timing is the key. Devote a few minutes to your Special each day and you will be rewarded with large dividends.

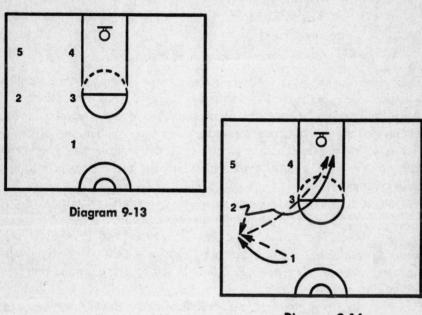

Diagram 9-13

Diagram 9-14

Multiple-Scoring Plays from the Jump-Ball

Tactically, securing possession of the basketball by means of the many jump-ball situations is often neglected. Since every possession puts your offense in motion, the jump-ball situation should be thought of as another means of scoring. An average of eight to 10 jump-ball situations occur in every game, and that could be 20 additional points.

With more coaches using various jump training programs in hopes of increasing the vertical jump of their players, it should only be logical that more emphasis be placed on obtaining possession on each jump-ball situation.

Team organization for control of the jump-ball is very important for overall team and coaching success. As with your out-of-bounds plays, you should try to score off the jump-ball if the situation warrants it. Therefore, you should first plan on controlling the tap and then be prepared to score with an organized play. In addition, you should use the fast-break principles of filling the lanes and alleys in hopes of gaining an advantage situation.

Basic Rules on Jump-Balls

- Try to gain control of the tap.
- Try to obtain a pinch situation (two of your players side-by-side).
- When your opponents have the advantage, have a designated defensive man back.
- Use fast break principles of filling lanes and alleys.

These rules should be stressed early in the season so that players are familiar with the strategy of the jump-ball situation. Since the beginning of the game, the quarters and the halves start with the jump-ball, serious consideration for gaining possession should be given to the jump-ball situation. Strong offensive and defensive play at both ends of the court will result in more jump-balls each game, providing justification for stressing the importance of the jump-ball situation.

Since this book is based on offensive techniques, only some of the multiple-offensive plays in jump-ball situations are covered.

Jump-ball plays should be simple by design and easy to execute. Each player on your team should be allowed to practice all phases of the jump-ball situation. Particular attention should be given to gaining possession and maintaining control.

Basically, there are three jump-ball alignments: the box, the diamond and the Y. If your opponents have a distinct advantage at the circle, you should employ the Y formation as a *defensive* formation. The three basic formations are illustrated in Diagrams 9-15–9-17.

The Box Screen-Opposite Tap

In the Box formation, Diagram 9-18, player 3 will tap to 5. Player 4 sets a screen on the opponent's player between himself and player 2. Player 2 then sprints hard toward the goal, looking for the pass from 5. Player 1 rotates to his right after the ball is tossed by the official. This serves two purposes. First, if the opponent's jumper attempts a back tap, player 1 is in position to intercept the ball. Second, player 1 must be in position to slow up any fast-break transition attempts by the opponents. This play can be mirrored if 3 taps to 4. After the pass to player 2, player 5 fills the left lane, with players 3 and 4 filling the left and right alleys respectively.

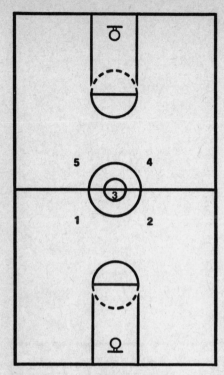

Diagram 9-15
The Box

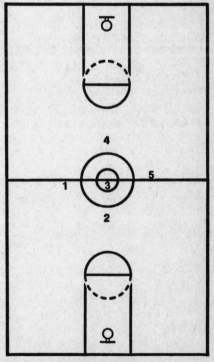

Diagram 9-16
The Diamond

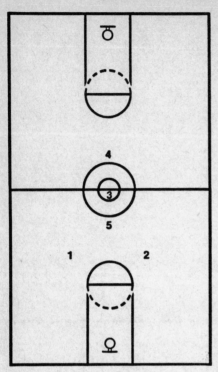

Diagram 9-17
The Y

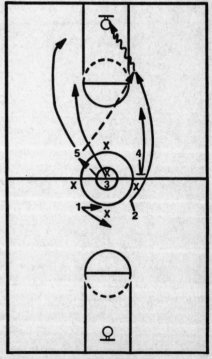

Diagram 9-18

The Diamond Double-Screen

The Diamond Double-Screen (Diagram 9-19) is a multiple option play starting with a tap to player 4, who is the best retriever. If your opponent does not have a deep defender, this play will be more effective. After the tap, players 1 and 5 set screens on the defenders next to player 2. Player 2 chooses his own route to the goal. He does this by reading the defense. Player 4 looks and hits 2 if he is open. Again, the players assume their respective lane and alley responsibilities with 1 staying back for defense. Players 3 and 4 fill the alleys and 5 fills the left lane.

The second play from the Diamond formation is illustrated in Diagram 9-20. Player 3 taps to either 1 or 5. Player 4 sets a screen on the opposing jumper, with 3 streaking to the goal and looking for a pass from the wing player who retrieved the tap. Player 4 then fills the left alley, players 1 and 5 fill the lanes on their respective sides and 2 stays back for defense.

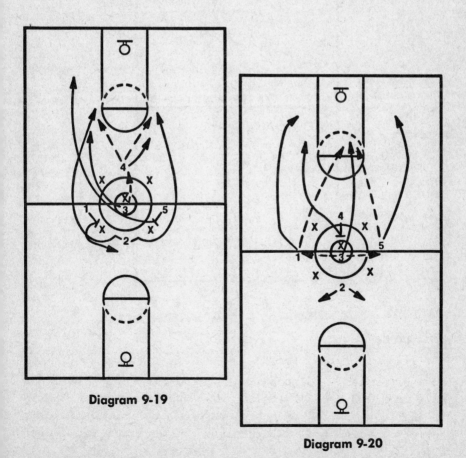

Diagram 9-19

Diagram 9-20

The Y-Formation and Fast Break

The fast break play from the Y-Formation is illustrated in Diagram 9-21. The Y-Formation is probably the most common *defensive* alignment, but if you obtain possession, a quick score can result. Player 3 back-taps to player 5, with 4 screening for either player 1 or 2. Player 5 then makes a lob-pass to the wing who was screened for. Player 3 fills the left alley with 1 in the left lane if he wasn't screened for. Player 4 fills the right alley with 5 staying back for defense. Players 1 and 2 exchange fast-break assignments depending on who is receiving the lob-pass from 5.

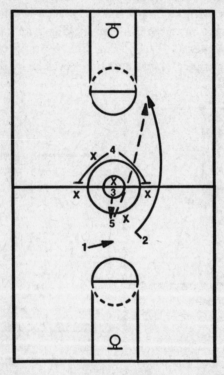

Diagram 9-21

The Squeeze

The Squeeze play can be used at any of the three jump circles when you feel you will clearly be outjumped, but need possession badly. You should make sure that all of your players are between your opponents and on the same side (right or left). You should leave obvious openings, inviting the tap to the open area. When the ball is tossed, rotate (all clockwise or counter clockwise) to the area in hopes of intercepting what your opponents think will be an easy possession. (Diagram 9-22)

These plays are easy to learn and execute. They can make the difference in a close game, but in order for them to be successful, you must provide practice time in your daily schedule to insure sound execution.

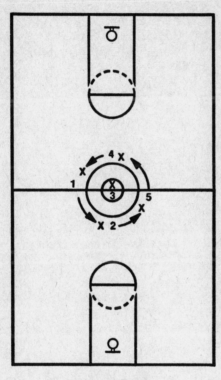

Diagram 9-22

10

Drills for Developing Offensive Proficiency

The Importance of Fundamentals

The mastering of fundamentals is the true foundation for developing winning basketball teams. Fundamentals development is one phase of basketball that must not be overlooked. The conscientious coach can help himself by creating a "Madison Avenue" campaign in selling not only the role, but also the need for the sound development of basketball fundamentals.

In stressing the importance of fundamentals, introduce them early and build upon them. The reduction of individual and team errors will develop a necessary ingredient for winning—*confidence.*

In developing fundamentals, adhere to the part method, progressing to the whole method as the players become more proficient in their skills. Start with the basics, review and then advance. Through this process, the players gain great individual confidence, because they are not asked to digest too much, too soon. The offensive drills you will use, while familiar to many, will play an important role in your success because they are applicable to the total offensive phase of basketball.

It is extremely important for you to display a sincere belief in fundamental basketball. Your players must sense that you have a genuine concern for, and are knowledgeable about, basketball fundamentals.

If you introduce a fundamentals-oriented program early, and in an organized manner, you will not only be rewarded with your players' confidence, but also with successes. This chapter describes several drills used to develop fundamentals. These and other drills throughout this book will be the major factors in your overall success.

Non-Dribble Series

Drill #1: Fingertip Passing

Procedure: The player's arms are held out straight, about even with the shoulders, and the ball is passed quickly between each hand using only the finger tips. The ball should be moved from over the head to the waist and from the waist back to the starting position.

Drill #2: Circle the Body

Procedure: The Circle The Body Drill is illustrated in Diagram 10-1. Each player, starting at his waist, circles the ball up to his head and down to his ankles. He should reverse the procedure and start again for a total of thirty seconds.

Drill #3: Circling Each Leg Separately

Procedure: The Circling-Each-Leg-Separately Drill illustrated in Diagram 10-2 is a progression drill from Drill #2. Each player, while keeping his head up, circles the ball around his right leg. On your whistle, the players perform the same movement around their left leg. The time for this drill should be about fifteen seconds for each leg.

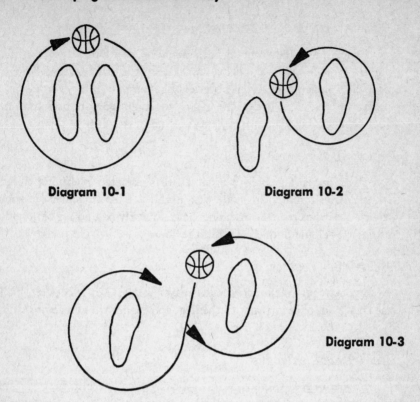

Diagram 10-1   Diagram 10-2

Diagram 10-3

Drill #4: Figure Eight

Procedure: The popular Figure-Eight Drill is shown in Diagram 10-3. To complete one rotation, the player moves the ball through the legs with the right hand, and with his left hand, it is now carried around and in front of the left leg. Now, the player, using his left hand, continues the procedure between his legs with the right hand being used to circle the ball around the right leg and back to the original starting position. The drill is reversed allowing fifteen seconds in each direction.

Drill #5: Switch

Procedure: The Switch Drill is an excellent hand reaction drill. It begins with each player maintaining a parallel stance, with the ball held between the legs. One hand is in front and one hand is in back. On your whistle, the players switch hand positions quickly and under control, while not permitting the ball to hit the floor.

Drill #6: Front-to-Back Bounce-Catch

Procedure: The Front-to-Back Bounce-Catch Drill is excellent for developing hand reactions and overall quickness. The drill is executed by having the player bounce the ball once between the inside of his legs while catching the ball in back of his body. The ball is then bounced from back to front and caught again. Thirty seconds is plenty of time for this drill.

Drill #7: Ball in Front

Procedure: The Ball-in-Front Drill is executed by having the player hold the ball in front of his body with his arms extended and about shoulder height. He drops the ball, claps his hands quickly behind his back and then catches the ball in front before it hits the floor.

Drill #8: Ball Between Legs

Procedure: In this drill, each player releases a ball between his legs, claps his hands once in front of either leg, and catches the ball before it hits the floor.

Drill #9: Slap the Thighs

Procedure: Each player throws a ball underhand into the air, slaps his thighs in front once and catches the ball in front of his body. The progression continues when the player tosses the ball again and slaps his thighs twice. To continue further, the player throws the ball in the air again and slaps his thighs as many times as possible, still trying to catch the ball before it hits the floor. This drill can be made competitive by having the coach buy a coke after practice for the player who makes the most slaps.

Dribble Series

Drill #10: Whirl-Around

Procedure: The Whirl-Around Drill starts with each player in a seated position and with his legs stretched out. On your whistle, the player begins with a right-hand dribble, bringing the ball around his back to his left hand. He then dribbles with his left hand around his legs to his right hand. This drill should be executed for about thirty seconds.

Drill #11: Double-Dribble

Procedure: The Double-Dribble Drill is an excellent drill for the development of hand-eye coordination, agility and ball control. Have three players line up at one end-line, each in one of the lanes, and each with two basketballs, one in each hand. On the whistle, the players alternately dribble the balls to the other end and back. This drill will progress slowly, but as the alternating skill is practiced, the players will ultimately be able to nearly sprint-dribble up and back without losing control. Stress concentration and control in the beginning.

Drill #12: Dribble-Reverse and Pivot

Procedure: The Dribble-Reverse-and-Pivot Drill is illustrated in Diagram 10-4. Rubber pylons are set up to extend from foul-line to foul-line and slightly staggered. Players line up behind the first pylon. The drill starts with the first player dribbling and as he reaches each pylon, he executes a reverse-pivot with his dribble, switching hands so that he is dribbling with his outside hand. It is important that the ballhandler uses the hand that is to the outside of the defender. As each ballhandler reaches the last pylon, he reverse-pivots again and speed-dribbles back to the end of the line. The second player starts as the first player is midway through the pylons, and so on.

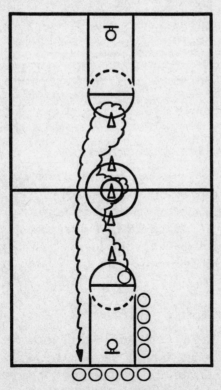

Diagram 10-4

Drill #13: Four-Corner Dribble, Pivot and Pass

Procedure: The Four-Corner Dribble, Pivot and Pass Drill (Diagram 10-5) is an excellent drill that incorporates dribbling, pivoting, passing and pass-catching. It may be used as a warm-up drill. The players are positioned with 1 starting the drill by dribbling towards 2. As soon as 1 reaches the far free-throw-lane line, he makes a flip-pass to 2, who meets the pass. Player 2 passes back to 1 who executes an inside pivot and passes to 2, who is heading for player 3. Player 3 steps out to receive the pass and follows the same procedure. Player 4 then repeats the set with the next player in line 1. Players move to the line to which they pass.

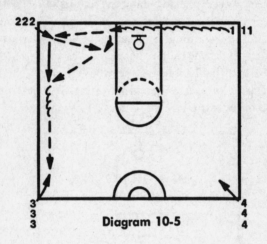

Diagram 10-5

Drill #14: Dribble, Jump-stop, Pivot and Pass

Procedure: The players are positioned as shown in Diagram 10-6 with the first four players possessing a ball. On your whistle, each player dribbles out to the foul-line, jump-stops, pivots and passes back to the next man in his line. He then returns to the end of the line. The points of emphasis in this drill are on ball control, keeping the ball low, and pivoting as fundamentals. Two-handed chest-passes should be used first and then an over-the-head pass as the drill progresses.

Drill #15: Full-Court Reverse-Dribble

Procedure: The Full-Court Reverse-Dribble Drill teaches the players to keep their heads up while dribbling and to reverse-dribble. It is also a good guard-release move to execute in order to avoid a defensive player prior to the start of any of your attacks.

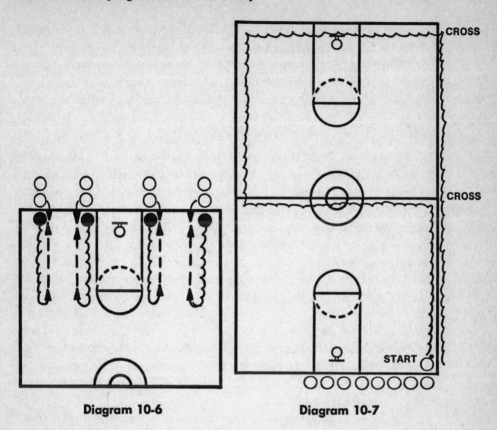

Diagram 10-6   **Diagram 10-7**

Each player has a ball and is lined up at one end of the court as seen in Diagram 10-7. The first player starts his dribble up the sideline and upon reaching mid-court, executes a reverse-dribble by pivoting on his left foot, swinging his right leg in an exaggerated hooking maneuver and finishes the move at a 225 degree turn. Hooking the defender is important because we want the defense on your hips, away from the ball.

At this point you should decide which is best for your players, to complete the move with the same hand or change dribbling hands after pivoting. Many coaches want their players to change hands because it may help eliminate ball handling violations.

After the first player completes his first reverse, he continues dribbling on the mid-court stripe toward the opposite side line. When he reaches this line he pivots on his right foot, crosses his dribble to his left hand and continues to the endline. When he reaches the endline, he pivots on his right foot and continues dribbling with his left hand to the opposite sideline. Upon reaching this sideline, player 1, pivots on his right foot again, and crosses his dribble to his right hand as he proceeds to midcourt. At midcourt, he crosses his dribble to his left hand and dribbles to the end of the line.

When player 1 pivots the first time at mid-court, the second player starts, and when he reaches midcourt, the next player starts and so on. The up and back movement keeps the players' heads up to avoid collisions.

Drill #16: Cross-Over Dribble and Shoot

Procedure: The Cross-Over Dribble and Shoot Drill is depicted in Diagram 10-8. The cross-over maneuver is especially effective in trying to evade a defender. The squad is divided into two groups with at least two balls in group two. A chair or pylon should be used at first to simulate a defender. Later, players in group two can play defense as well as rebound. The drill starts with the first player in line two executing a two-hand chest-pass to the first player in line one. Player 1 starts dribbling towards the chair and as he nears the chair, the cross-over move is made. As his foot on the dribbling side contacts the floor, player 1 pushes off hard toward the opposite foot. His dribbling hand is kept low and slightly outside of the ball, while angling it across his body for the opposite hand to continue the dribble. A long cross-over step by the foot on the original side of the dribble is executed to complete the maneuver. In order to keep the defender off-balance, the change-of-direction must be emphatic. Stress the importance of keeping the ball low in order to minimize a deflection or steal.

As player 1 completes the cross-over maneuver, he continues his dribble and drives toward the basket, where he takes a layup or a short jumper. Player 2 rebounds and the players exchange lines.

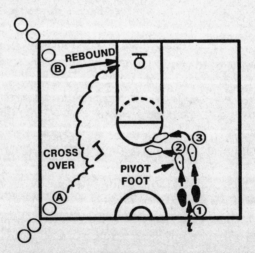

Diagram 10-8
Dribble Push off pivot foot Long cross-over step

Drill #17: Full-Speed Spin, Dribble And Shoot

<u>Procedure:</u> The Full-Speed Spin, Dribble and Shoot Drill is illustrated in Diagram 10-9.

The spin move is very effective against a defender who has good position on the ball side. However, caution is advised in using this maneuver against double-team tactics because the dribbler completes the move with his back to his defender and is vulnerable to weakside defensive help.

Player 1 receives a pass from player 2 and dribbles toward the chair. As he nears the chair, the spin move is executed. While dribbling hard to the chair, player 1 jump-stops, pivots on his left foot and swings his right leg around in a 225 degree turn. A big turn of the right leg is necessary so that the dribbler can hook the chair (defender) and keep the defender on his right hip.

The dribbler keeps his right hand dribble instead of changing hands, and the move must be executed quickly while keeping the defensive man away from the ball. As player 1 maintains his dribble, he continues to the basket and shoots a layup or short jumper. We use the spin move as part of our continuity pre-game warm up routine.

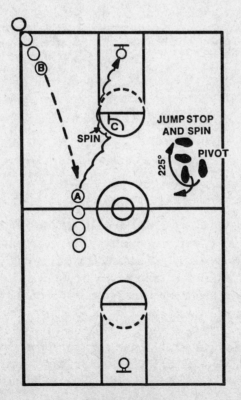

Diagram 10-9

Drill #18: Rocker-Step and Drive

Procedure: The Rocker-Step and Drive Drill is shown in Diagram 10-10. The squad is divided into two groups with player 2 passing to player 1 and coming out to defense him to start the routine. As player 1 receives the pass and is confronted with the defender, he steps toward the basket as if to drive. If defender 2 retreats, player 1 draws back his stepping foot, straightens upright and brings the ball into shooting position.

If the defender advances, player 1 places his stepping foot next to the defender's advanced foot and drives hard to the basket. It is imperative that the driver make his first move next to and outside of the defender's advanced foot because in order for the defense to catch the offensive man, he would have to drop his advanced foot completely backward, thus providing an open alley to the basket. Execute this drill from both sides of the key.

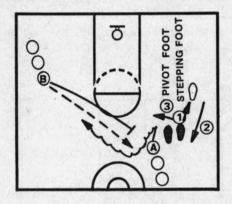

Diagram 10-10
Step Back to start Cross over and drive

Drill #19: Jab-Step And Drive

Procedure: The Jab-Step and Drive Drill in Diagram 10-11 is similar to the rocker step. The jab-step, however, is a short, quicker move and for that reason more coaches are teaching it in place of the rocker-step.

The players are lined up as they were for the Rocker-Step And Drive Drill. The first player in line two passes to the first player in line one and comes out to play defense. Player 1 attacks the defender with a quick back-straightening move, followed by a second, short, six-inch thrust of the non-pivot foot. It is this quick short thrust or jab that puts the offensive player in an advantage position. If he jabs to his right, he will use his right foot to lead with and his left foot as his pivot. If he jabs left, he will lead with his left foot using his right foot as his pivot. In both instances, the offensive man protects the ball by placing it on the hip to which he is making the jab-step.

The reaction of the defender dictates what offensive move will follow. If the defender gives ground, the offensive man can shoot or drive to his strongside for a close-in shot.

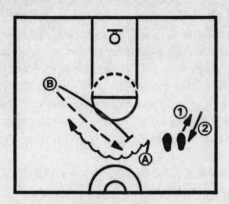

Diagram 10-11
6" jab Back to start

Another maneuver that the offensive man can perform is to bring his jabbing foot back to the original position, Diagram 10-12, cross his right leg to the left side while placing the ball on his left hip and drive with his left hand to the basket. (Diagram 10-13) At all times, the offensive player must keep his body between the defender and the ball.

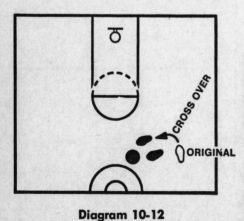

Diagram 10-12

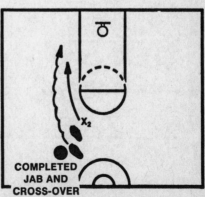

COMPLETED JAB AND CROSS-OVER

Diagram 10-13

Passing

Drill #20: Two-Line Passing

Procedure: The Two-Line Passing Drill (illustrated in Diagram 10-14), develops hand and eye coordination, quick release, accuracy in passing, and it makes the players meet each pass. The team is divided into two single lines that are facing each other approximately twelve to fifteen feet apart. The first player in line one executes a two-handed chest pass and follows this pass, cutting to either side of the receiver. The first man in line two steps up to take the pass and gives a return flip pass to player 1 as he goes by and to the end of line two. Player 1 then gives a flip pass to the next player in line two. Player 2 continues and goes to the end of line one.

Drill #21: Rapid-Fire Passing

Procedure: The Rapid-Fire Passing Drill (Diagram 10-5) is very good for the development of peripheral vision. Divide your squad into equal groups of at least six players per group. Two balls are needed for each group. One player with a ball is stationed about ten feet from the group and faces it. One player in the group has a ball. As the lone player in the middle passes to a member of the group, the other ball is passed to him. The balls are then moved up and down the line continuously. Rotate your players so each man has a chance in the middle.

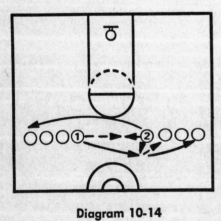

Diagram 10-14

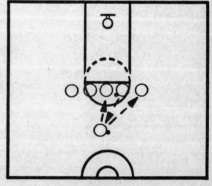

Diagram 10-15

Drill #22: Wall-Pass Catching

Procedure: The Wall-Pass Catching Drill develops hand-eye coordination and pass catching ability. The squad is divided into groups of two, with each group having a ball. Player 1 has his back to the wall and stands about eight feet from it. Player 2 stands with the ball off to one side and throws the ball high, low, middle and with varied strength. Player 1, must pivot when he hears the ball hit the wall and tries to catch it before it bounces. When he catches the ball three consecutive times the players switch positions. This drill helps a player who has "bad hands". (Diagram 10-16)

Drill #23: Four-Corner Dribble, Pivot and Pass

Procedure: This drill teaches dribbling in short bursts, jump-stopping, pivoting and passing. The squad is divided into four groups with the first player in each group having a ball. The drill starts with the first four players dribbling to the top of the key, coming to a jump-stop, pivoting on their right foot and passing to the line directly opposite them after their pivot. A two-handed chest pass is used and each player proceeds to the end of the line he passed to. When the timing in this drill is perfected, all the players will be dribbling, jump-stopping, pivoting and passing in unison. (Diagram 10-17)

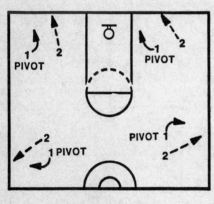

Diagram 10-16

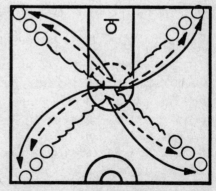

Diagram 10-17

Drill #24: Four-Corner Passing

<u>Procedure:</u> The Four-Corner Passing Drill (Diagram 10-18), is part of our regular pre-game warmup routine. The drill focuses on quickness, accuracy in passing, timing and pass-catching reaction. The squad is divided into four groups in one half of the court. Player 1 passes to player 2 and moves toward him for a return pass. Player 1 then passes to 3 and proceeds to the end of line 3. Meanwhile, player 2 cuts off 1, receives a pass from 3, passes to player 4 and goes to the end of line 4. Player 3, meanwhile, cuts off 2, receives a pass from 4 and passes to the next man in line one. He then proceeds to the end of line one. The second player in line two cuts behind 4, receives a return pass from the second man in line two and passes to the second player in line three and so on. Before going full speed, have your players walk through this drill several times.

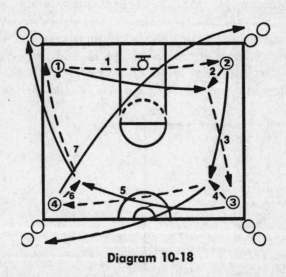

Diagram 10-18

Drill #25: Four-Corner Pass and Shoot

<u>Procedure:</u> The Four-Corner Pass and Shoot Drill (Diagram 10-19), teaches passing, timing, meeting the ball, pivoting, pass-catching and shooting. Line one starts the drill with the first player executing a two-hand chest pass to player 2, who breaks to meet the pass. Player 2 pivots on his left foot and executes a two-hand over-the-head pass to player 3 who is coming to meet the pass. Player 3 pivots on his left foot and executes a bounce-pass to player 4. After 1 passes to player 2, he cuts behind 2 and breaks for the basket, receiving a bounce pass from player 4. Player 1 may take a left-handed layup or a short bank-shot. Player 4 rebounds the shot and pitches out to player 2 at the

free-throw line. Player 2 now pivots and passes back to the next player in line one. The players exchange lines by going behind the line to which they first passed. Use two balls to keep the drill alive.

Drill #26: Four-Man Passing

<u>Procedure</u>: The Four-Man Passing Drill (Diagram 10-20) is a passing drill as well as a great conditioner. Four designated players are used to start the drill and are positioned on each side of the two foul lines. Two to four balls may be used. The first player in line steps out and executes an over-the-head pass to Player 1 and then sprints to mid-court. Player 1 then pivots and executes an over-the-head pass back to the first player, who executes the same pass to player 2. Player 2 pivots, spots the first player cutting to the basket after a change-of-direction move and hits him in the lay-up position with a bounce pass. The shooter rebounds his own shot and repeats the same procedure on the opposite side. The second player in line goes after the second pass. This drill should be used for a duration of time and with four new players out un the court. This drill involves a lot of passing and player movement and

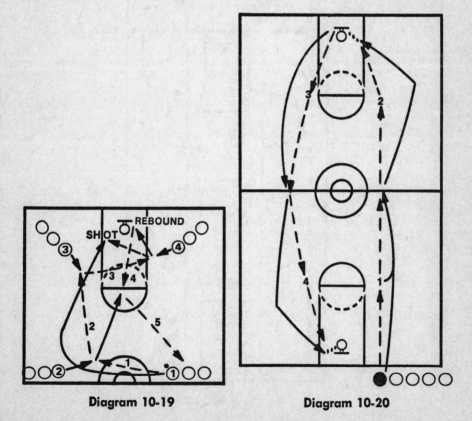

Diagram 10-19   Diagram 10-20

should be kept under control with a firm emphasis on the fundamentals being stressed.

Drill #27: Full-Court Head Passing

   <u>Procedure:</u> The Full-Court Head Passing Drill culminates a two-on-none or two-on-one fast break situation. In Diagram 10-21, the players are placed into four groups with the players on the inside having the basketballs. This drill can also be executed with two groups of three players or one group of three players with one or two balls. On your whistle the two inside players quick-pass the ball to the two outside men and move ahead to get a return pass. The drill continues the full length of the court with the players passing back and forth until they reach the opposite end. The next group starts when the first group reaches mid-court. After all the groups have gone, they return, following the same procedure. This drill is run with a time duration which

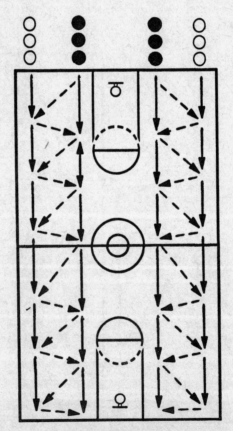

Diagram 10-21

emphasizes timing, hand-and-eye coordination, peripheral vision and crisp passing on the move with each player's head up.

Drill #28: Full-Court Press-Breaker Pass-and-Cut

Procedure: The Full-Court Press-Breaker Pass-and-Cut Drill (Diagram 10-22), is a great conditioner as well as incorporating all of the pass-and-cut movements of our press offense. This drill should be used with a time duration and the players should run it several times before changing positions or before a new group steps onto the court. There is absolutely no dribbling allowed in this drill.

Player 5 starts the drill with a pass to 1, who breaks to the ball after a change-of-direction move. All of the players must use a change-of-direction move before meeting each pass. Player 1 pivots and hits 2 breaking into the middle lane. Player 2 then pivots and hits 5 moving down the third lane. By this time, player 3 is in the 3-lane and takes player 5's pass. Player 2 is heading for the 2-lane, player 4 is shuffle sliding into the low post, player 1 heads for the ballside and 5 sets up opposite 1 for the swing series. After 3 takes 5's pass,

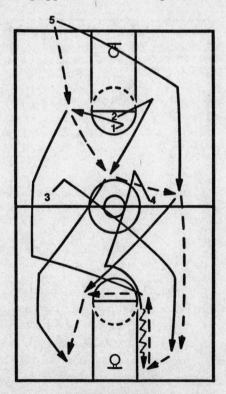

Diagram 10-22

he hits 4 in low. Player 4 pivots and passes out to 1 who swings the ball to 5 and 5 hits 2 in the 2-lane. Repeat the drill until you're satisfied with the execution.

Pass-and-Shoot

Drill #29: Four-Corner Pass-and-Shoot

Procedure: The Four-Corner Pass-and-Shoot Drill emphasizes passing, timing, jump-stopping and shooting. The squad is divided equally into four groups. Player 1 starts the drill by passing to 4, using a two-handed chest-pass. Using an over-the-head pass, player 4 passes to the first player in line 2. Player 2, using a two-handed chest-pass hits 3 near the foul-line. Player 3 must use a change-of-direction move before taking 2's pass. Player 3 takes the pass with a jump-stop, squares his shoulders to the basket and shoots the 15-foot jumper. Rotation: 1 to 4, 4 to 2, 2 to 3 and 3 retrieves his own shot and goes to the end of line 1. (Diagram 10-23)

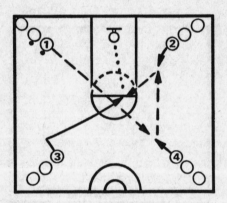

Diagram 10-23

Drill #30: Change-of-Direction Move, Pass-and-Shoot

Procedure: This is an excellent drill that incorporates passing, moving without the ball, cutting and shooting. The team is divided as shown in Diagram 10-24 with players 1 and 2 having a basketball. Player 3 uses a change-of-direction move to the lane and comes back to the ball, taking 1's pass. Player 4 uses a change-of-direction move down to the baseline, comes back and takes a pass from 2. Players 1 and 2 get return passes and drive to the basket for the power layup. After shooting, players 1 and 2 cut toward the sideline in their respective ends of the court. Players 3 and 4 rebound the shots and outlet the balls to 1 and 2. Players 1 and 2 pass to the next man in line and the procedure continues. A special emphasis should be placed on the importance of good, accurate and strong outlet passes.

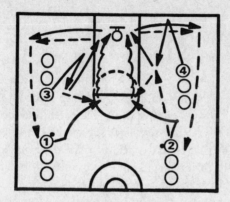

Diagram 10-24

Drill #31: Big Man

Procedure: The Big-Man Drill (Diagram 10-25) is a great hustle drill for post players. Two balls are used and the drill starts with the first player in line 1 passing to the first player in line 2. The players in line 2 must use a change-of-direction move before coming to the ball. After taking the initial pass, the players in line 2 use either a lob- or bounce-pass to the post, who shoots turn-around-jumpers. The players in line 2 rebound and pass to the next man in line 1 and go to the end of line 1. The players keep the post men

Diagram 10-25

moving with quick passes, forcing them to shoot with rapid-fire action. After about a dozen shots a new post man is used and the drill continues. The players in line 1 rotate to the 2 line. The drill should also be used on the opposite side of the court.

Layups

Drill #32: Speed-Dribble with Power Layups

Procedure: The Speed-Dribble with Power Layup Drill (Diagram 10-26) teaches the players how to shoot the power layup after speed-dribbling. Divide the team into two groups: dribble-shooters and rebounders. The drill can start from either the right or left side, but whichever side the dribblers are on, you should instruct them to dribble with their outside hand. The drill starts with all the dribblers maintaining their dribbles. On the coach's whistle, the first player in line speed-dribbles with his left hand to the foul line extended. At this point, he begins to shuffle-slide into the layup position by putting his right leg forward on an oblique angle and then sliding to the

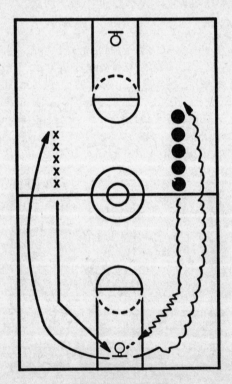

Diagram 10-26

basket. The shuffle-step allows the dribbler to maintain control of his movements, and it also places any would be defenders on his back. From this side, the layup should be taken with the left hand. The execution on the right side is just the opposite from the left. The rebounder, on the shot, shouts "shot," then blocks out the shooter, and upon possession shouts "ball." The rebounder then dribbles to the shooting line and the shooter moves to the rebounding line. The drill is then executed from the right side.

Drill #33: Reverse Layup

Procedure: The Reverse Layup Drill (Diagram 10-27) is similar to Drill #32. Start on the left side because most players are right-handed and you want them to gain confidence in their weak hand. With all the players in the left line maintaining their dribbles, the first player dribbles up to the first defender (X) near the foul-line extended. Here, he protects the ball with a low cross-over dribble and hooks the defender's left leg with his left leg and continues to the basket, taking a right-handed reverse layup. The defender, who applies only token defense rebounds and dribbles back to the shooting line. The shooter becomes the defender-rebounder.

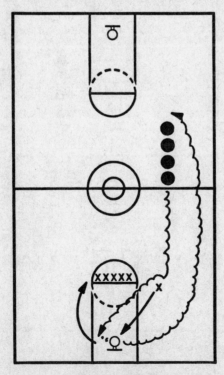

Diagram 10-27

Drill #34: Reverse-Dribble and Layup

Procedure: The Reverse-Dribble and Layup Drill (Diagram 10-28) is an important ball-handling and layup-shooting drill. The layup down-the-middle is one of the most difficult shots in basketball. It can be a shot that culminates a cutting move, or it can be at the end of a fast break. In any event, it is a shot that is missed too often. If the shooter comes straight in, he should lay the ball up just over the front rim after he comes to a jump-stop. The jump-stop is the key to making this shot because the shooter is able to maintain body control instead of continuing out-of-bounds as he shoots on the run.

The drill starts with the dribbler penetrating with his right hand. As he nears the defender, he hooks the defender's right leg with a drop-step, using his right leg, and completes the reverse-dribble and layup in front of the rim. The defender-rebounder blocks, rebounds and dribbles the ball to the shooting line.

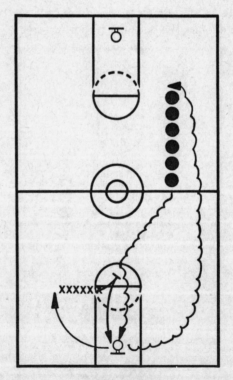

Diagram 10-28

Drill #35: Full-Court Layups

<u>Procedure</u>: The Full-Court Layup Drill (Diagram 10-29) emphasizes dribble control, passing and shooting the power layup. The squad is divided at mid-court. On your whistle, Player 1 dribbles with his left hand and Player 7 dribbles with his right toward their respective baskets. As 1 and 7 shoot their layups, Players 6 and 10 rebound the shots and pass to Players 2 and 8. Rotation: 1 behind 12, 6 behind 9, 7 behind 4 and 10 behind 3. Remember, have your players jump-stop with both feet and go up-and-in to the basket.

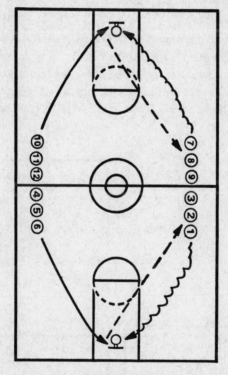

Diagram 10-29

Shooting

Drill #36: Three-Line Dribble, Pass and Shoot

<u>Procedure</u>: The Three-Line Dribble, Pass and Shoot Drill (Diagram 10-30) is an excellent warm-up drill that incorporates passing, cutting,

dribbling, rebounding and shooting. The team is divided into three groups at mid-court. Two balls are used and the middle line starts the drill. As 1 moves out, player 2 executes a two-hand chest-pass to him. Player 1, using his left hand, dribbles in and makes a left-handed power layup and rebounds his own shot. Player 1 now bounce-passes to 3, cutting in for a right-handed layup. Player 1 rebounds 3's shot and passes to 2 at the foul-line for a 15-foot jump shot. All three players then get into rebound position, and if 2 misses, they tip the ball until it goes through the net. The next three players in their lines continue the drill. Players rotate to their right.

Drill #37: Follow Your Shot

Procedure: Getting players to follow their shots can be an exasperating chore. This drill (Diagram 10-31) helps instill the "follow your shot" idea in the player's minds. The squad is divided into equal groups at both ends of the court. One player in each group is up, shoots and follows his shot. After retrieving his shot he passes to his partner who follows the same procedure. An

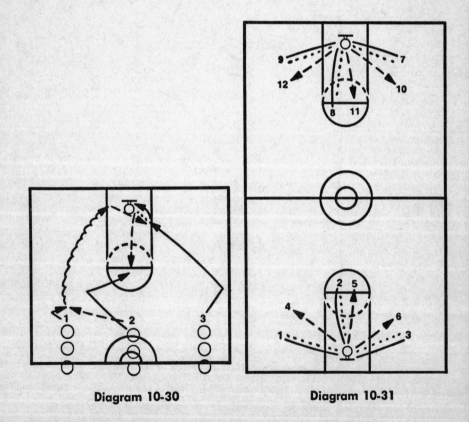

Diagram 10-30   **Diagram 10-31**

important point for the shooters is to establish a pivot foot when shooting. If the player moves to his right, then his left foot is his pivot foot. If he moves to his left, then his right foot is his pivot foot. This drill should be used for a duration of time.

Drill #38: Competitive Shooting

<u>Procedure</u>: The Competitive Shooting Drill (Diagram 10-32) is an excellent drill that focuses on quick shooting and accuracy. The team is divided into groups of three, each group being one team. Allow the players to take almost any shot, providing it isn't wild or impractical. Group 1 starts the drill with the first player selecting his shot from any spot at his basket. The remaining groups must follow the same procedure. The shooter retrieves his own rebound and passes back to the next player in line on his team. Ten baskets must be made before the groups rotate (clockwise) to the next basket where they are to make ten more. This procedure is continued until a group has returned to its starting basket. More than one group may be at a basket as each team tries to catch and pass the others.

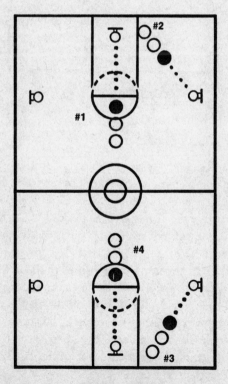

Diagram 10-32

Drill #39: Drive and Jump-Shot

Procedure: This drill is easy to organize and execute and should be used everyday. Its basic teaching point is shooting off the dribble, a very important fundamental. The drill is set up in Diagram 10-33. The O's being the shooters and the X's the passer-rebounders. On your signal, the X's pass to the O's who take one or two quick but hard dribbles to their right or left depending on floor position, and take the jump shot. The X's rebound the shot and return the balls to the shooters who continue to shoot until the coach makes a change. The shooters should rotate to different offensive spots before coming out of the drill.

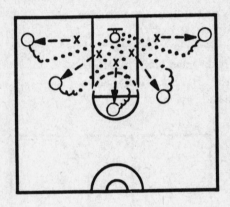

Diagram 10-33

Drill #40: Nine-Minute Shooting

Procedure: The Nine-Minute Shooting Drill (Diagram 10-34) is an excellent drill that incorporates shooting, passing and rebounding. Quick shooting and accuracy should be emphasized. Players 1 and 2 have basketballs. Player 1 is the first shooter, player 2 is the passer and 3 is the rebounder. Each shooter shoots for 55 seconds. The players then get 5 seconds to rotate.

The drill starts with the 1's shooting from the right corners. The 2's immediately pass to the shooters who continue to shoot. The rebounders (3's) retrieve the shots, pass to the 2's and the 2's continue passing to the shooters (1's). Rotation: 1 to 3, 3 to 2, 2 to 1. After all the players shoot from the right corner, the first shooters shoot from the top of the key area and after another rotation, shoot from the left corner. All players shoot from all three spots, taking a total of nine minutes for shooting and rotation. The two main baskets and two side baskets should be used.

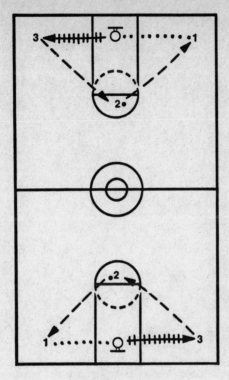

Diagram 10-34

Index

A

Advantage situation, 132
Alley, 135

B

Backdoor:
  Clear-Out Series, 51
  Spread 1-2-2, 83
Backdoor series:
  Basic Inside-Out Attack, 38–39
  1-4 attack, 66
Ball advancement principles, 153–154
Ball between legs drill, 196
Ball-in-front drill, 196
Ball-Reversal Maneuver, 94–95
Bank shots, 68
Baseline series:
  attacking zone defenses, 100
  Basic Inside-Out Attack, 33–35
  double low-stack, 76–79
  1-4 attack, 60–67
Baseline series drill, 42–43
Basic Inside-Out Attack:
  Clear-Out Series related, 46
  continuity and offensive moves, 30–35
    double low-stack alignment, 35
    getting into baseline series, 33–35
    guard through, 34
    "jam-it" to big man, 33
    penetrating low post, 30
    pick-and-roll, 31
    post man roll-and-exchange, 33–34
    undercutting with wing guard, 31–33
  drills, 41–43
    baseline series, 42–43
    hitting the stack, 42
    pick and roll, 41

Basic Inside-Out Attack (*cont.*)
  End-of-Period Offense, 39–40
    "hope shot," 39
    "quick popper," 39
    rotating into stack, 39
  initiating with guard entries, 26–30
    hitting the stack, 29
    hitting the side post, 28
    hitting the wing, 26–28
  Inside-Out vs. any defense, 21–22
  personal placement and description, 22–23
  rebound responsibilities, 40–41
  relieving guard pressure, 37–39
    backdoor series, 38–39
    post screen-and-roll, 38
    wing guard screen, 37
  strongside, 23
  versatility of offense, 24–26
  weakside, 35–37
    hitting the stack, 35–36
    reversing to wing, 37
Big man drill, 211–212
Big men, 58
Box-and-one, 112
Box formation, 180–181
Box screen-opposite top, 186

C

Change-of-direction drill, 147–148
Change-of-direction move, pass-and-shoot,
  210–211
Circle the body drill, 194
Circling-each-leg-separately drill, 194
Clear-out:
  continuity pattern, 51–52
  1-4 attack, 57
Clear-Out Series:
  auxiliary man-for-man attack, 45

Clear-Out Series (*cont.*)
  continuity pattern, 51–54
    clear-out, 51–52
    scissor, 53–54
  related to Inside-Out Attack, 46
  relieve guard pressure, 49–51
    backdoor, 51
    posting low, 49–50
    two-man pick-and-roll, 49
  reverse action, 55–56
  weak defense, 47–48
Combination zones, 91–115
Coming-over-the Top, 60
Competitive shooting drill, 217
Continuity pattern, 51–54
Controlled fast break:
  advantages, 128
  advantage situation, 132
  alley, 135–136
  drills, 138–149
    change-of-direction, 147–148
    11-man continuity, 148–149
    fast-break progression, 138
    five-man fast break, 142
    four-man series, 141
    fundamentals, 142–149
    head-pass, 146–147
    Player 1, 142, 144
    round-robin, 145–146
    three-man progression, 138, 140
    three-on-two, 144–145
    two-on-one, 144–145
  fast break factors, 130–131
  non-advantage situation, 135
  organizing, 129–137
  personnel requirements, 131–132
  psychological effect, 128
  starting, 130
  swing-pass series, 136–137
Cross-over dribble and shoot drill, 200
Cuts, 97

D

Diamond-and-one, 112
Diamond double-screen, 189
Double-dribble drill, 196–197
Double Low-Stack:
  advantages, 71
  against man-for-man, 71
  against zone defenses, 71
  alignment, 35

Double Low-Stack (*cont.*)
  baseline series, 76–79
    post roll-and-exchange, 76–77
    reversing to wing, 77–79
  Basic Inside-Out formation, 70
  big men close to basket, 71
  continuity offense, 71
  disadvantages, 71
  entire offensive series, 70
  establishing strongside, 72–73
  excellent offensive rebounding, 71
  fewer people handle ball, 71
  fewer turnovers, 71
  getting into, 70–73
  high-percentage scoring, 71
  "jamming-it" to low post, 74–75
  minimum of passes, 71
  mirrored from either side, 71
  multiple formations, 70
  not for entire game, 71
  not physically tiring, 71
  offensive keys, 71–72
  penetration by point guard, 71
  pick-and-roll, 75
  players' responsibilities don't vary, 70
  quick-shot offense, 71
  rebound responsibilities, 84
  relieving guard pressure, 79
  screening by post man, 72
  susceptible to fast break, 71
  timing vital, 71
  use, 71
  weakside cut over-the-top, 75
  wing guard behind post man, 70
Double-option bomb, 168–171
Dribble, jump-stop, pivot and pass drill, 198
Dribble-reverse-and-pivot drill, 197
Dribble-reverse maneuver, 96
Dribble series drills:
  cross-over dribble and shoot, 200
  double-dribble, 196–197
  dribble, jump-stop, pivot and pass, 198
  dribble-reverse and pivot, 197
  four-corner dribble, pivot and pass, 198
  full-court reverse-dribble, 198–200
  full-speed spin, dribble and shoot, 201
  jab-step and drive, 202–203
  rocker-step and drive, 202
  whirl-around, 196
Drills:
  ball between legs, 196
  ball-in-front, 196
  baseline series, 42–43

Drills (*cont.*)
  Basic Inside-Out Attack, 41–43
  big-man, 211–212
  change-of-direction, 147–148
  change-of-direction move, pass-and-shoot,
    210–211
  circle the body, 194
  circling-each-leg-separately, 194
  competitive shooting, 217
  controlled fast break, 138–149
  cross-over dribble and shoot, 200
  double-dribble, 196–197
  dribble, jump-stop, pivot and pass, 198
  dribble-reverse-and-pivot, 197
  dribble series, 196–203
  drive and jump-shot, 218
  11-man continuity, 148–149
  fast-break progression, 138
  figure-eight, 195
  fingertip passing, 194
  five-man fast break, 142
  follow your shot, 216–217
  four-corner dribble, pivot and pass, 198, 205
  four-corner pass-and-shoot, 206–207, 210
  four-corner passing, 206
  four-man passing, 207–208
  four-man series, 141
  front-to-back bounce-catch, 196
  full-court head passing, 208–209
  full-court layups, 215
  full-court press-breaker pass-and-cut, 209–210
  full-court reverse-dribble, 198–200
  full-speed spin, dribble and shoot, 201
  head-pass, 146–147
  hitting the stack, 42
  importance of fundamentals, 193–194
  jab-step and drive, 202–203
  layups, 212–215
  nine-minute shooting, 218–219
  non-dribble series, 194–196
  pass-and-shoot, 210–212
  passing, 204–210
  passing game, 109–112
  pass-screen opposite, 109
  pick-and-roll, 41
  Player 1, 142, 144
  post-screen-post, 110
  rapid-fire passing, 204
  rear-screen continuity, 111
  reverse-dribble and layup, 214
  reverse layup, 213
  rocker-step and drive, 202
  round-robin, 145–146

Drills (*cont.*)
  shooting, 215–219
  slap the thighs, 196
  speed-dribble with power layups, 212–213
  step-in or replace, 109–110
  switch, 195
  three-line dribble, pass and shoot, 215–216
  three-man progression, 138, 140
  three-on-two, 144–145
  two-line passing, 204
  two-on-one, 144–145
  wall-pass catching, 205
  whirl-around, 196
Drive and jump-shot drill, 218

E

11-man continuity drills, 148–149
End-of-period offense, 39–40
Even front, 98, 99–104

F

Fast break, 127, 190
  (*see also* Controlled fast break)
Fast-break progression drills, 138
Figure-eight drill, 195
Fingertip passing drill, 194–196
Five-man fast break, 142
Flash-cut, 61–62
Follow your shot drill, 216–217
Four-corner dribble, pivot and pass drill, 198, 205
Four-corner pass and shoot drill, 206–207, 210
Four-corner passing drill, 206
Four-man passing drill, 207–208
Four-man series, 141
Four-option continuity play, 181–182
Front-to-back bounce-catch drill, 196
Full-court head passing drill, 208–209
Full-court last-second shot, 183
Full-court layup drill, 215
Full-court man-for-man pressure, 163–171
Full-court press-breaker pass-and-cut drill,
    209–210
Full-court reverse-dribble drills, 198–200
Full-speed spin, dribble and shoot drill, 201

G

Guard clear, 66

Guard cut:
  1-3-1 zone defense, 123–124
  zone defenses, 103–104
  zone-press offense, 157–158, 162–163
Guard entries, 26–30
  Basic Inside-Out Attack, 37–39
  Clear-Out Series, 49–51
  Double Low-Stack, 79
Guard through, 34
Guard to post, 82
Guard to wing guard, 81

H

Half-court last-second shot, 183
Half-court pressure, 172–176
Head-pass drill, 146–147
High 1-4, 98
Hitting the stack, Basic Inside-Out Attack, 29–30
Hitting the stack drill, 42
Hitting the wing, 26–28
"Hope shot," 30
Horizontal play, 178–179

J

Jab-step and drive drill, 202–203
"Jam-it" to the Big Man, 33, 103
"Jamming-it" to low post, 74–75
Jump-ball, 185
Jump hook, 61
Jump-shot, 61

L

Laning zones, 91
Layup, 61
Layup drills:
  full-court, 215
  reverse, 213
  reverse-dribble and layup, 214
  speed-dribble with power, 212–213
Low post, 30–31

M

Man-for-man attack, auxiliary, 45
Man-for-man full court pressure, 163–171
Man-for-man pressure, 183

Matchup zones, 105–109
(*see also* zone defenses)
Medium 1-4, 98

N

Nine-minute shooting drill, 218
Non-advantage situation, 135
Non-dribble series drills:
  ball between legs, 196
  ball in front, 196
  circle the body, 194
  circling each leg separately, 194
  figure eight, 195
  fingertip passing, 194
  front-to-back bounce catch, 196
  slap the thighs, 196
  switch, 195

O

Odd-front zone, 98
Offensive principles, 92
Offensive rebounding, 67–68
1-4 attack:
  alignment, 58
  backdoor maneuvers, 57
  baseline series, 60–67
    backdoor series, 66
    flash-cut, 61–62
    from high post, 65–67
    guard clear, 66
    post roll-and-exchange, 62–63
    rear screen, 62
    rebound responsibilities, 66
    reversing to weakside, 60–61, 63–64
    strongside post roll-and-exchange, 64
  big man, 58
  changing starting point, 58
  clear-outs, 57
  establishing strongside, 59
  from high post, 58
  from medium post, 58
  half-court man-for-man pressure, 172–173
  half-court zone pressure, 174–176
  little weakside defensive help, 57
  man-for-man full-court pressure, 163–167
  offensive rebounding, 67–68
    bank shots, 68
    fakes occupy defenders, 68
    positioning, 67
    roll-off, 68
    teammates' shooting habits, 68

1-4 attack (*cont.*)
  1-3-1 zone defense, 117–126
  (*see also* 1-3-1 zone)
  personnel placement, 58
  pick-and-roll, 60
  point man with four entry passes, 57
  post men, 58
  quick shot, 57
  shot or 1-on-1 drive, 59
  three-second violation, 58
  what it does, 57
100 series, 124–125
1-3-1 passing game, 105–109
1-3-1 zone:
  1-4 versus, 118–124
    advantages, 119–120
    guard cut, 123–124
    initiating guard entries, 120–124
    pass to strongside post, 121–122
    pass to strongside wing, 120
    pass to weakside post, 122–123
    pass to weakside wing, 120
    100 series, 124–126
    pass to pivot, 125
    pass to wing guard, 124–125
  popularity, 117–118
  rebound responsibilities, 126
Open key
(*see* Spread 1-2-2)
Out of bounds, 177
Overloading, 94

P

Pass-and-shoot drills:
  big man, 211–212
  change-of-direction move, pass-and-shoot,
    210–211
  four-corner pass-and-shoot, 210
Passing drills:
  four-corner, 206
  four-corner dribble, pivot and pass, 205
  four-corner pass and shoot, 206–207
  four-man, 207–208
  full-court head, 208–209
  full-court press-breaker pass-and-cut, 209–210
  rapid-fire, 204
  two line, 204
  wall-pass catching, 205
Passing game, 93, 105–112
Passing lanes, 94
Pass-screen opposite drill, 109
Pass to pivot, 125

Pass to safety, 158, 160
Pass to strongside post, 121–122
Pass to strongside wing, 120
Pass to weakside post, 122–123
Pass to weakside wing, 120–121
Pass to wing guard, 124–125
Personnel, fast break, 131–132
Personnel placement, 1-4 alignment, 58
Pick-and-roll:
  Basic Inside-Out Attack, 31
  Clear-Out Series, 49
  double low-stack, 75
  1-4 attack, 60
Pick-and-roll drill, 41
Pivot, pass, 125
Player 1, drill for, 142, 144
Point to wing guard, 99–100
Positioning, 67
Posting low, 49–50
Post Man Roll-and-Exchange, 33–34
Post men, 58
Post roll-and-exchange:
  attacking zone defenses, 101
  Baseline Series, 62–63
  double low-stack, 76–77
Post roll cut, 97
Post screen-and-roll, 38
Post-screen-post drill, 110
Practice organization, 184
Presses, zone, 92
Pressure, relieving, 83
Pressure defenses:
  ball advancement principles, 153–154
  full-court man-for-man, 163–171
  half-court, 172–176
  keys for defeating zone presses, 154–155
  psychological outlook against, 152–153
  use, 151–152
  zone-press offense, 155–163
    basic alignments, 155–157
    guard cut, 157–158
    guard cut from stack alignment, 162–163
    pass to safety, 158, 160
    swing series, 160, 161, 162
    weakside flash, 158
  zone-press offensive tempo, 154

Q

"Quick Popper," 39–40
Quick shot, 57

R

Rapid-fire passing drill, 204
Rear screen, 62
Rear-screen continuity drill, 111
Rebounding, offensive 67–68
Rebound responsibilities,
   Basic Inside-Out Attack, 40–41
   double low-stack, 80
   1-4 attack, 66
   1-4 versus 1-3-1 zone, 126
   Spread 1-2-2, 84
Relieving guard pressure, 79
Replace drill, 109–110
Reverse action, 55
Reverse-dribble and layup drill, 214
Reverse layup drill, 213
Reversing to weakside, 60–61, 63–64
Reversing to wing:
   attacking zone defenses, 101
   Basic Inside-Out Attack, 37
   double low-stack, 77–79
Right-angle cut, 97
Rocker-step and drive drill, 202
Roll-off, 68
Round-robin drill, 145–146

S

Scissor, 53–54
Screening:
   post man, 72–73
   proper footwork, 29
Scrimmage games, 111–112
Shooting drills:
   competitive, 217
   drive and jump-shot, 218
   follow your shot, 216–217
   nine-minute, 218–219
   three-line dribble, pass and shoot, 215–216
Side-out series, 181
Slap the thighs drill, 196
Sliding zones, 91
Special, 184–185
Special situations:
   full-court last-second shot versus man-for-man
      pressure, 183–184
   home run, 183
   jump-ball, 185–191
      basic rules, 186
      box screen-opposite tap, 186
      diamond double-screen, 189
      squeeze, 190–191

Special situations (*cont.*)
   jump-ball (*cont.*)
      Y-formation and fast break, 190
   out-of-bounds, 177–183
      box, 180–181
      half-court last-second shot, 183
      horizontal play, 178–179
      player positions, 178
      side-out series, 181–182
      stack play, 179
      vertical play, 179–180
   practice organization, 184–185
      special, 184–185
Speed-dribble with power layup drill, 212–213
Spotting up, 104
Spread 1-2-2:
   against even-front zones, 98
   basic information, 80
   delay-game offense, 84–88
      advantages, 84
      alignment and continuity, 85–88
      apply pressure to defense, 85
      best ballhandlers, 85
      crisp passes, 85
      double team, 85
      easty to learn, 84
      15-foot spacing, 85
      highest-percentage shots, 84
      high-percentage shots, 85
      little dribbling, 84
      moving without ball, 85
      pass receivers, 85
      players without ball, 84
      poise, 85
      rules, 85
      team passing offense, 84
      when to use, 84
   guard to post, 82
   guard to wing guard, 81
   open key advantages, 80
   rebound responsibilities, 84
   strongside entries, 80–81
   weakside entries, 82–83
      backdoor, 83
      identical keys, 82–83
      relieving pressure, 83
Squeeze play, 190–191
Stack play, 179
Stack vs. box-and-one, 113–115
Step-in drill, 109–110
Straight cut, 97
Strongside:
   Basic Inside-Out Attack, 23

Strongside (*cont.*)
   double low-stack, 72–73
   1-4 attack, 59
   spread 1-2-2, 80
Strongside post, 121–122
Strongside post roll-and-exchange, 64
Strongside wing, 120
Stunting zones, 91
Swing-pass series, 136–137
Swing series:
   full-court man-for-man pressure, 168
   zone-press offense, 160, 161, 162
Switch drill, 195

T

Three-line dribble, pass and shoot drill, 215–216
Three-man progression drill, 138, 140
Three-on-two drill, 144–145
Triangle-and-two, 112–113
Triangular passing, 94
Two-line passing drill, 204
Two-man pick-and roll, 49

V

Vertical play, 179–180

W

Wall-pass catching drill, 205
Weak defense, 47–48
Weakside:
   Basic Inside-Out attack, 35–37
   cut over-the-top, 75
   1-4 attack, 60–61, 63–64
   Spread 1-2-2, 82
Weakside flash, 158
Weakside post, 122–123
Weakside series, 102
Weakside step-in, 101–102
Weakside wing, 120–121
Whirl-around drill, 196
Wing guard:
   pass, 124–125
   undercutting, 31–33
Wing guard screen, 37

X

X-cut, 97

Y

Y-formation and fast break, 190

Z

Zone defenses:
   ball fakes before passing, 90
   behind the defense, 90
   bounce passes, 90
   box-and-one, 112
   changes game tempo, 90
   combination, 91, 105–115
   crisp passes, 90
   diamond-and-one, 112
   15-foot spacing 90
   formations, 98–105
      baseline series, 100
      Basic Inside-Out, 99–104
      guard cut, 103–104
      "jam-it" to big man, 103
      point to wing guard, 99–100
      post roll-and-exchange, 101
      reversing to wing, 101
      spotting up, 104
      weakside series, 102
      weakside step-in, 101–102
   from 18 feet out, 90
   from inside 18 feet, 90
   fundamental concepts vs., 93–97
      ball-reversal maneuver, 94–95
      developing passing lanes, 94
      overloading and triangular passing, 94
      passing, 93
      penetration 95–97
      post roll cut, 97
      pressure high and low posts, 95
      straight or right-angle cut, 97
      X-cut, 97
   high-percentage shots, 90
   inside game first, 90
   laning or stunting, 91
   matchup zones, 105–109
      dribble rulers, 106–107
      general rules, 107
      1-3-1 passing game offense, 105–109
      passing rules, 106
      perimeter-player rules, 108–109
      post-player rules, 107–108
   offensive principles, 92
   overhead pass, 90

Zone defenses (*cont.*)
  passing game, 109–112
    pass-screen opposite drill, 109
    post-screen-post drill, 110
    rear-screen continuity drill, 111
    scrimmage games, 111
    step-in or replace drill, 109–110
  players in foul trouble, 90
  presses, 92

Zone defenses (*cont.*)
  stack versus box-and-one, 113–115
  standard sliding, 91
  triangle-and-two, 112, 113
  types, 91–92
  why used, 90
  zone offense, 89–90
Zone press offense, 154–163
(*see also* Pressure defenses)